Patristic Theology

Volume 1—2024

Contents

KEVIN M. CLARKE, JAMES R. PAYTON JR., AND DON SPRINGER
Introducing *Patristic Theology*   1

J. A. MCGUCKIN
Classical and Byzantine Christian Notions of the Self and
their Significance Today   6

CHARLES E. HILL
Enthroned upon the Cherubim: Irenaeus's Gospel
Symbolism and its Christological, Biblical-Theological,
and Codicological Ramifications   22

KEVIN M. CLARKE
Patrology beyond Suspicion: Hermeneutics, Holiness,
and Hope   65

TARMO TOOM
Hermeneutics in Augustine's *De Doctrina Christiana*
Books Two and Three   101

SEUNG HEON (HOSEA) SHEEN
St. Augustine's Number Pneumatology   135

Senior Editors
James R. Payton, Jr.
Don Springer

Associate Editor
Kevin M. Clarke

Editorial Board
Paul Blowers, Milligan University
Megan DeVore, Colorado Christian University
Amy Brown Hughes, Gordon College
John McGuckin, Oxford University
Brian Shelton, Asbury University
Clifton Ward, Covenant College
Robin Darling Young, Catholic University of America

Patristic Theology, a peer-reviewed academic journal produced by the McMaster Divinity College, publishes research on that rigorously engages early Christian texts and the theological wisdom that inspired them. As an open-access, peer-reviewed journal, *Patristic Theology* benefits the larger academy by providing an important venue for the publication of patristic theological research of the highest quality. The journal is published by the Centre for Patristics and Early Christianity (CPEC) at McMaster Divinity College. This research centre promotes the study of the texts and traditions of the mothers and fathers of the early church: their literature, theology, history, worship, and spirituality.

Articles are posted on the McMaster Divinity College website (https://mcmasterdivinity.ca/journals/patristictheology) and at the end of the year, the volume is available in hard copy as well. Manuscripts should be sent to PTJournal@mcmaster.ca.

Content of *Patristic Theology* is copyright by McMaster Divinity College, Hamilton, ON, Canada.

Introducing *Patristic Theology*

Kevin M. Clarke
Sacred Heart Major Seminary, Detroit, MI, USA

James R. Payton, Jr.
McMaster Divinity College, Hamilton, ON, Canada

Don Springer
McMaster Divinity College, Hamilton, ON, Canada

Patristic Theology is an open-access, peer-reviewed journal publishing essays both online and in print, offering scholarly studies on the teaching, faith, practice, and spirituality of Christian antiquity. The Centre for Patristics and Early Christianity, established by McMaster Divinity College, publishes *Patristic Theology*. The review process is blind. All essays, even solicited ones or essays by the editorial team or review board, are subject to review. Prior to an essay's being sent out for review, the editors will ensure that it is rigorously researched, well-formatted, and aligned with the publisher's style. To ensure a speedy review for an essay, authors should ensure that posted guidelines are followed closely.

Patristics journals are numerous, as are theological journals, but patristics journals that sustain a tight theological focus are indeed few, as many scholars have observed. Yet, this is the primary interest of a very large segment of scholars in the field. Hence, *Patristic Theology* sees its fit within the broader literature in responding to and providing for this need. The journal's name clearly indicates its subject matter, as the journal is specifically patristic and deliberately theological.

Patristic—The patristic era includes roughly the first eight centuries of Christian history following the age of the Apostles, or, generally speaking, from the Apostolic Fathers to John

Damascene. The word "patristic" derives from the Greek word for "father," and has typically referred to the study of the received Fathers of the Church, namely those who bore the four distinguishing marks of orthodoxy, holiness of life, antiquity, and Church approval. The editors of the journal do not intend the word "patristic" to restrict the scope of the journal. Rather, it should refer more broadly not only to the Fathers but also to significant theologians of early Christian history, including women. In this light, the editors especially encourage essays that explore the role of the "mothers" who helped shape the development of theological wisdom. Also of interest to the journal are those significant patristic thinkers sometimes referred to as ecclesiastical writers—those early Christian thinkers who may be theologically suspect in some way or another but who nonetheless present significant theological offerings worth considering here.

Theology—The journal aims to maintain a theological focus, in the same spirit as the subjects it will consider in its pages. The Spirit of God lived and moved in the early church as it does today. The age of the Fathers saw the continued spread of the Gospel throughout the world, the formation of the canon of the Scriptures, the flourishing of Biblical interpretation, the crafting of early apologetics, the trial of the earliest persecutions, the rise of a Christian empire, the gathering of ecumenical councils and the crafting of creedal definitions, the development of unique expressions of Christian worship through the various liturgical and prayer traditions, the advent of monasticism, the creation of a Christian culture and way of life, and much more. The growth of theological speculation in the early centuries of Christianity calls for rigorous research. A close consideration of the individual Fathers of the Church reveals an abundance of unanswered questions and pathways for theological research.

It is vital that theology have its own spaces dedicated to the advancement of theological truth and wisdom. While the work published in other patristics journals is significant for the field of patristics, theology often receives insignificant attention. *Patristic Theology* provides the space for the focused treatment and development of theological topics and themes as it pertains to the Fathers.

The editors welcome contributions along the following lines:

Scriptural topics—the interpretation of specific Biblical texts by the Fathers, the formation of the Scriptural canon, patristic engagement with extra-Biblical sources of theology, Scriptural commentaries or homiletics, the methods employed by the Fathers in the interpretation of Scripture, the senses of Scripture, controversies over Biblical interpretation, the authorship of Scripture according to the Fathers, patristic critiques of heterodox interpreters, etc.

Doctrinal topics—Trinity, Christology, pneumatology, salvation and deification, patristic accounts of Christian anthropology, the ecumenical councils and canons, grace and sin, creation, Mariology and the veneration of the saints, philosophical foundations for doctrinal issues, heresiology, Scripture's role in the development of any of the above topics, etc.

Ethical topics—Christian living and the commandments, the virtues and vices, asceticism, almsgiving, martyrdom and witness, repentance and restoration to communion, marriage and virginity, wealth and poverty, moral interpretations of Scripture, evangelization and mission, catechumenal instruction, theological discourse and polemics between Christians and non-Christians, stewardship of creation, pastoral ministry, etc.

Ecclesial topics—unity in diversity in the early Church, the interplay between universal and particular churches in the patristic era, the ordained ministries, the rise of the pentarchy, the liturgical identity of various patriarchal churches, the "domestic Church" or ecclesial life in the home, the early church building as a sacred space, the "marks" of the church, the iconographic tradition, etc.

Worship, spirituality, and mystagogical topics—the rise of the Christian liturgy, rites of Christian initiation, monasticism, communal prayer life, pious practices such as pilgrimages, women's communities and spirituality, the *logismoi* and the interior life, patristic influence upon the liturgy, feasts and relics, growth in holiness, early prayer, theurgy, etc.

General topics—who are the Fathers, who else ought to be considered a Father, theological evaluation of patristic categories, the Fathers and their literary genres (poetry, sayings, hagiography, historical theology and the theology of history, early historiography, autobiography, etc.), patristic critique of secular culture, etc.

Translations—Original translations of shorter patristic works are welcome. Translators should clearly indicate the original text from which they are translating so that those reviewing the translation may examine it closely.

Possibilities are not limited to the above. These broad guidelines are obviously not exhaustive. Essays fit with the journal to the extent that they are both patristic and theological. Essays only tangentially related to patristic theology are unlikely to be accepted. Permissions to reproduce any copyrighted material, such as the author's own published material, critical texts, or images, are the author's responsibility. Authors should receive editorial permission prior to submission of any essay that has already been published. Generally, such works will not be accepted. Previously published material must be substantially updated in order to justify publication. The submission of any essay for review means that the essay is not under consideration elsewhere and adheres to all ethical norms concerning academic publishing.

At this stage, the editors have no plans to receive books for review. As the journal grows, this possibility may be revisited from time to time. In the meanwhile, response essays evaluating significant works of patristic theology are welcome to be submitted, though such essays, unless invited, will be subject to the ordinary review process. Until such time as the journal receives and distributes books, it will be up to the author to acquire the book, as there will be no guarantee of publication. Book copies for invited reviews will be coordinated between the editors, the prospective author, and the publisher.

We welcome your readership and encourage all contributions that support the journal's aims and mission. Progress in patristic theological discourse is good for Christian unity. Thus, the journal seeks to be truly ecumenical. The editors intend for the journal throughout its life to become a vibrant locus of *Ressourcement* in the West, wherein the voices of early Christians and those of our contemporaries engage in a sustained discourse. May God grant it length of days. Let the conversation begin.

CLASSICAL AND BYZANTINE CHRISTIAN NOTIONS OF THE SELF
AND THEIR SIGNIFICANCE TODAY[1]

J. A. McGuckin
Oxford University, Oxford, United Kingdom

Personhood as a Concept under Threat

We may tend to think today that the concept of the human person (and here I mean the term philosophically, the idea of spiritual subjectivity) is the unassailable focus of our Christian culture, the locus of some of our highest religious and intellective ideals, and the last bastion of the concept of social and political freedom. Even if we are aware of the revisioning of ideas of self that goes on apace in the worlds of cyber science, often called "Artificial Intelligence," we might think that this cannot assail the primacy of the place the idea has in our culture. But the same changes are also going on with great energy in the field of contemporary neuroscience. Here, new empirical understandings of the complexities of the brain have newly raised old questions about identity and personhood, once approached in the light of metaphysics and philosophy.

The movement around personality and personhood is not entirely in the direction of materialist reductionism, however. The old arms-length distance that science formerly employed, to hold away what they saw as the "suspicious" trades of the theologian and philosopher, have begun to be eroded more rapidly in this era than at any other time since the sixteenth century. And this is something of a problem, because formative training in the long ages of the great divorce we have witnessed between arts and

---

[1]. A lecture offered to the "Andrei Saguna" Faculty of Theology at the University of Sibiu (Romania), on the occasion of the bestowal of an Honorary Fellowship and a *Doctoratus Honoris Causa*.

sciences have rendered theologians unskilled in scientific method and produced generations of scientists who are rank amateurs in terms of philosophy—who now need philosophical rigour to advance beyond the frontier of the investigation of the brain's chemo-electrical synaptic functioning, so as to arrive at significant statements about personhood beyond the simple mapping of personality disorders. The same applies equally for physicists, to allow them to go beyond the long accepted impasse of two systems for explaining cosmological rule-ordering, so as to approach the single pressing question of the disparities of cosmic existence, one that might offer a coherently comprehensive account of *what it is that is*—which is, I suggest, the provoker of that other great metaphysical question which never goes away: *why it is that anything is at all?*

So, unquestionably we need today to learn new sets of languages. One common term of semantics that lies in our midst—a security checkpoint, as it were, between the armed camps of humanities and sciences; between religion and secularism; between philosophy and metaphysics; between the microcosm and the macrocosm—is the concept of the person.

This concept, we may think, is so central to all European thought, so basic to an understanding of everything significant, that we may even be tempted to take it for granted. We ought not to make that mistake. For most of the history of the idea "personhood" was not significant at all as a substantive—certainly not in the worlds of the great antique religious systems.[2] And in those systems of religion and philosophy that still follow the archaic matrices, such as Hinduism or Buddhism, this is still the case. Far from being a substantive, personhood is approached at best as an accidental, at worst as a deceit—*Maya*, that illusion of personal identity that prevents the seeker after truth from recognizing the structures of reality.

---

2. As Philip Cary puts it, "Human beings can describe themselves in emotional, ethical, and religious terms, without recourse to the conception of a private inner world. Indeed, before Augustine, everyone seems to have found it natural to do so, having no notion that there was an alternative" (*Augustine's Invention*, 9).

In the pre-Christian classical systems of cosmology which emphasized cyclical schemes of coming to being and coming into dissolution, personhood was an accidental category, and so it occupies a place in Aristotle's scheme of the natural order. One cannot derive a sure knowledge of the *genus* by application of so peripheral a notion as the individual (*to idion*). One needs to make an analysis of the *ethos* of the whole nature (*ousia*) by reference to its *teleotic* drive. The *telos* or the end goal of the nature, seen as an enclosed and driven system, renders the fractured approach of personalist understandings wholly irrelevant. *Prosōpon*, the Greek word for "person" (a thing which misleads so many readers of textbooks today), does *not* mean person in our sense of discrete subjective consciousness; it simply refers to an existent specimen—*to idion*. The semantic itself gives the game away, for *prosōpon* derives from the Greek for an actor's megaphone—the mask or "face" the classical actor wore on stage (with fixed clichéd aspects of happiness or sorrow or fear) to serve as an amplification system for the audience. *Prosōpon* was itself a cliché of singularity, not a mark of individuation. *Persona* is simply the Latin synonym, and *per sonare* literally means an actor's speaking tube.

It was the Christians, however, who brought this idea of the centrality of personhood, the new concept of the substantive nature of the person, to the fore in human culture and thought; and it was Christians who in the age of Byzantium supplied the new and refined semantic for one of the greatest advances in thought about human consciousness that history records. *Prosōpon* became *hypostasis*. It was Christological and Trinitarian doctrine that drove this process on. I would like to focus on this in the first part of this presentation in order to draw some conclusions about what this might suggest to us in an age when the very place of personhood in centre stage on world philosophy and science is being attacked by twin forces of dissolution: first of all, the negative energy of a culture no longer understanding the value-systems society holds up for itself (this was why classical antiquity, rooted in a mythical system of values, fell before Christian logic); and secondly, the darker force of mechanization of the human spirit that seeks to reduce those unexpected and often uncontrollable brilliances of human individual spiritedness into a system that can depersonalize sufficiently, so as to enable collectivization and thus control. We have lived through a so-called "great age" in the last two centuries—not so much the great age of empire (as they fell too frequently in the course of time for that) but rather the so-called great age of *totalitarian collectivization*. These twin forces of value dissolution and mechanized collectivism operate relentlessly in human society—sometimes taking on a savage and dark form and oppressing generations at a time, when the energy of a totalitarian leader puts collective power to work subjugating persons; but sometimes also in eras of great social "drift" when the laziness of a society neglects its philosophical axioms, grows apart from or distant to them, and allows the great inner core of notions such as freedom and philanthropy to corrode and give ground before the growth of non-personal philosophies. One case in point is western capitalism in a global environment, that much vaunted "defender" of the rights of individual persons, which has raised consciousness in the developed West to such a pitch (a point of narcissism, one might even say), but clearly at the cost of enslaving and silencing countless hundreds of thousands of others, who work in the sweat shops of the world unseen and unheard. Ours is the age, the third in line after imperial Rome, and then colonial America, when slavery has been reinvented. It is not the *résumé* we might expect for our contemporary civilization, to be sure, but global slavery has been estimated in our time as embracing a minimum of ten, and a possible upper figure of thirty, million people on the face of the earth in conditions of true enslavement.

If Christians first brought the notion of personhood as a substantive to the world's agenda, we might be in a position to repair the notion in a time when it is clearly being damaged by those who either do not understand its universality (and dismiss the rights of persons), or those who do not seem to understand its function as a term of communion (and so elevate rights of persons as a privatist agenda separated from broader terms of social and moral culture). Let me base these statements by looking first into Platonic, then Aristotelian, then Byzantine Christian philosophies of personhood, for it is my thesis that the Christian personalism of the Byzantines, their synthesizing response to the work of the classical philosophers, is that which today still underpins the Eastern Orthodox conception of transfigured humanity, and of society as communion, which many parts of western culture appear to have lost sight of, by having lost the intellectual premises out of which the philosophy of personhood first arose. This happened in four acts: two Platonic iterations, one Aristotelian, and an overarching Byzantine Christian synthesis prefigured by the classical patristic age.

Briefly put, the force of the concept of individuation for the Platonic system is that it is *a process of the ascent of the psyche to the Ideal, an epistemic journey, which is its liberation and return to primary form.* In the Aristotelian system, the idea of individual consciousness is used as *a process of moral expression. It is the emergence of the individual as free agent.* In the late revisions of both these Greek schools which we now call Neoplatonism, reflection on individuation becomes *a process of inward focus for connection to the intelligible realities that signal the mystical connection of the individual to the Supreme Nous.* Finally, the Christian Fathers synthesized this collective material and subordinated it to a fundamental soteriological principle of a divine incarnation into history transfiguring the bondedness of human reality (the mortal *ousia*) into a liberative *epektasis*, a bounded infinity of the mortal rendered immortal by entering the fathomless reality of communion with the infinite God.

Individuation in Pre-Christian Greek Thought

The Platonic school is fundamentally responsible for the success of that all-pervasive image of the self as the "true inner reality," a private and clarified place where the self emerges and the boundaries of the divine and human become to some degree tangential. In the *Phaedo*, Plato considers what is meant by the immortality of the soul. For him, the soul has a certain kinship with that which is everlasting, immortal, unchanging. It has the quality of an Ideal Form. Philosophical inquiry into the soul, and other aspects of the good life, is the empirical *praxis* of immortality: such enquiry strengthens the bond between the soul and the Ideal Forms with which it has kinship. In Homeric writing, the Soul or Osyche had been merely a fluttering and useless shade. For Plato, however, it is the adamantine core which frees itself from material limitation. To know the soul one must first know the Ideal Form.[3] The soul fell from the Ideal Forms and was imprisoned in material sensible reality. There is, thus, an important division between Intelligible and Sensible, between Ideal Form and material deformation, between Being and Becoming. True wisdom is gained by recollection of the knowledge that the soul possessed before its material decline. The way to this wisdom, Plato maintains, is by searching and true perception. This cannot be achieved if one already thinks (mistakenly) that one possesses a true perspective—a common illusion that suffocates humanity (his famous analogy of the prisoners in the cave).

Using Socrates as an ideal teacher, Plato begins with *aporia* ("puzzlement"), the systematic destruction of existing false premises, to arrive, by reduction and denial of false ideas, at a true conception (*orthos logos* or *orthodoxia*). The dialogue *Meno* pursues this track in seeking to define Virtue. The student of philosophy who begins to see is one who can eventually join with Socrates in setting puzzling questions himself—applying the aporetic method as a self-directed means of truth finding.[4] We already have the answer to what we seek; we need to stimulate the awareness of the Ideal Forms by Recollection. For this, he uses the verb *en-einai*—a "being in" or a "being possible." The point of the wordplay is that knowledge is possible for us because it is already in us. The dawning insight to which this reflective scrutiny leads us is a cardinal moment in philosophy and ethic, and it charts the emergence of self-knowledge.

Plotinos, the greatest of the Neoplatonic teachers, later married Platonist theories of divine intelligible reality with the Stoic moral motive of the inward turning to the life of the soul, thereby trans-

---

3. Gregory the Theologian, in his *Theological Orations* and his poem *Carmen Lugubre*, as well as Augustine later, in his *Confessions* and *De Trinitate*, will reverse this path by making psychology the path towards theological insight.

4. Thus, the path to wisdom is synonymous (in both classical philosophical thought and especially in the Byzantine ascetic fathers) with the path to the emergence of the True Self.

forming Platonic metaphysics into a viable religious system that had immense attraction for Christians. For Plotinos, the archetypal model of the eye of the soul is the Supreme *Nous*, or *The One*—that divine reality which is the centre of all Existence, the Unity which all multiplicity innately yearns for. The World-Soul, or *Logos*, mediator of this unity to the disparate cosmos, revolves around this supreme Light like a satellite moon. Because of this, individual souls (which are akin to *Logos*) also revolve around the light in their individual existences but are ambivalently capable of orientating towards that light or facing outward into the darkness of non-intelligible reality. If the soul turns towards the light, it turns inward by a natural kinetic energy to noetic awareness. The awareness grows, for the elite, to the point of noetic union—the mystical apprehension of reality as "One beyond the Many." Here, late Platonic metaphysics has become close to being a spiritual religion.[5] St. Gregory the Theologian is much affected by this model, whereas his historic mentor, Origen of Alexandria, was much closer to the older "ascentive epistemic" imagery of Plato. Both Origen and Gregory, however, differ considerably from their Platonic sources in the way that both of them constantly evoke the biblical idea of transfiguration (*metamorphosis*) as a way of explaining the human *telos*.[6] For both, the *Logos* is personified and personifying in a way that for Plotinos it is decidedly not.

Aristotelian Presuppositions

Aristotle, in seeking to approach the definition of reality from a different perspective to the intellective (noetic/spiritual) idealism of Plato, marked a new beginning for reflective thought on the nature of the individual. The Platonic system left more than a large question mark hanging over the very validity, or at least utility, of

---

5. St. Augustine, of all the Fathers, is the closest to the Neoplatonic idea of selfhood here, in that he prefers an image of an "inner palace" of the self where one can enter to find a potential encounter with God; the Greek fathers more thoroughly mediate Neoplatonist ideas of how *Logos* serves to mediate Supreme Reality to individual *logoi*.

6. Cf. the treatment in McGuckin, *Transfiguration of Christ*.

the scrutiny of contemporary existential forms (the sensible/sensory domain which was de facto illusory). For Plato, there was the perennial danger of mistaking the "shadow on the wall" of the cave for a perception into Ideal Form. With Aristotle, the concept of the *class*, or of *nature*, has become a dominant aspect of his taxonomy of existence. For him, it is the nature which is essential, and the individual which simply manifests it, or constitutes it "practically." The universal form, for Aristotle, was located within the collective character of the *genus*. Only here was a substantial form (*ousia*) capable of empirical description. Therefore, the close observation of the individual specimen, a serious empirical scrutiny, leads to the amassing of a clear understanding both of the generic class and the characteristics (accidents, *idiomata*) of the individual manifestation of that *genus*.

The key to this process of analysis of the substantial form was the study of *genesis*—that is, the manner in which a life form evolves, sets into motion its own peculiar and characteristic activities, and unfolds towards its natural *telos* ("goal"). The true definition of a thing is that which it is when it has attained the sum of its generic potential. This gave rise to a dynamic sense of nature as a "lived-out process." For Aristotle, *energeia* is that which moves the life form from potentiality to the perfected realization of its essence. For a human, the *bios*, the way a person directs the life force, is critically important. This is the very unfolding of the nature, not merely a product of it. Even in the Supreme Being the essence is an energy, an *actus purus*.[7] In the case of humanity, this process is the manner in which individuals, or "primary substances" as he describes them, unfold their life-force teleologically in the course of a life's activities, choices, and attainments—a teleological process which is the acquisition of human nature in the particular case of each individual, an arrival at authentic human nature which is only potentially present in individual members of the species from birth. It is, for example, from such arguments about teleology that Aristotle famously does not consider young people capable of moral identity—a position which was to

---

7. This was to have an immense impact on Latin medieval Christian thought, especially that of the great scholastic Thomas Aquinas.

be highly influential on Christian ascetics and their doctrine of the passions and *apatheia*.

In this system, the acquiring of a form of natural *stasis* ("stability"[8]) is quintessential to the emerging of true identity. In antique-biographical terms, the chief item of importance is the cataloguing of the accurate "empirical moment," that time and place and condition in which the *humanum* has finally emerged. Childhood and old age are not key areas of the Aristotelian reality of the person, as being chiefly conditioned by pupae-like emergence or senile decadence. This "attained" humanity is characterized as the *ethos* of a person. *Ethos* is a fundamental concept for Aristotle's thought, and it is a sought-after goal of much ancient autobiographical writing, seen as the depicting of the *ethos* of the self.[9] Aristotle's ideas were significant for drawing a strong connection in antiquity between a close psychological scrutiny and a program for moral *paideia* (educational philosophy). Philosophy in this genre was fundamental for defining anthropology and for attaining the goal of the *telos* of the *humanum*.

Christian Configurations of the Self

Clearly then, the purpose of Late Antique philosophy, pagan or Christian, in this era (that is, its *skopos*) was to embrace the issue of transcendentals. The Christians, among other schools of the time of the Second Sophistic, had a lively interest in matters of religious philosophy that had been left unresolved by the ancient greats. A prime example of this was Plato's theory of the soul's nature and the shape of its ascent. In terms of the former, Plato had left the philosophical tradition a dominant image of the Soul being somehow like a charioteer, and the way one resolves the problem of the chariot's direction being an *exemplum* of the good life. The soul-chariot is driven by two horses, one black (standing for the appetitive part of the soul, *to epithymitikon*), one white

---

8. The moral goal was *hexis*—the stable acquisition of virtue; it was seen as the natural expression of *arete*.

9. A key motivation in the first Christian autobiography, St. Gregory the Theologian's *De Vita Sua*.

(standing for the irascible part of the soul, *to thymikon*). The charioteer stands for the reasoning faculty in a human (*to logistikon*) who struggles to control the forces of the soul, especially the more unmanageable black steed. This appetitive soul is the part of human experience and consciousness driven by instinct, desire, and self-reference. The irascible soul is that which seeks nobler and more elevated forms in life. The principle of reason, or adjudication, tries to mediate between the two struggling "drives" that make up the *psyche*. It is a very lively image that held a great sway. It proposes the philosophical life as quintessentially the one which seeks to integrate human faculties, in a moral habituation that privileges higher things over base instincts, exemplifying the Socratic principle that the unexamined life is not worth living.

Now the Byzantine Christians, in the synthetic tradition of the Cappadocian Fathers' muted Origenianism, developed the Platonic psychology in a very distinct way that gave birth, in effect, to a vibrant new form of philosophical anthropology. Into Plato's strongly dyadic view (two horses pulling differently under the attempted mastery of the mind) they introduced more of a genuinely triadic structure to rework from its foundations the doctrine of the soul (*psyche*). While the Apostle Paul often spoke of the binary war of flesh (*sarx*) and spirit (*pneuma*), it was equally noticeable to the Fathers how the New Testament tended to address the issue of the constitution of the human as a triadic correlation of body, soul and spirit. This triad was brought into dialogue with Platonic "psychology" by the Fathers, beginning with Origen, so that the core of the human consciousness now became the lower soul (*epithymitikon*), the higher soul (*thymikon*), and the spiritual intelligence (*Nous*). Writers of the Origenian intellectual tradition—notably Gregory the Theologian, Evagrius Pontike, Maximus the Confessor, Dionysios the Areopagite, and Elias Ekdikos (along with many other monastic theorists)—applied this doctrine pervasively in the Byzantine world's ascetical theory of mystical contemplation. St. Gregory the Theologian habitually calls Christianity in general, and the ascetical life in particular, "our philosophy."

Among the Fathers, the lower soul was seen to be the body consciousness attuned to instinctive life. It had a range of needs and desires (fight/flight/acquisition) dominated by material concerns. It had also a range of perceptions, moving from simple material awarenesses (hunger, fear) to more elevated sensibilities (empathy, affection). At the top range of the lower soul's *skopos*, it overlapped with the lower range of the middle soul. The middle soul represented a more emotive and more abstracted range of consciousness (dealing in perceptions and deductions and higher questions of motivation), but it was still intimately linked with its lower neighbour—sometimes guiding it, sometimes being led by it. At the middle soul's upper range, however, it was akin to its next higher neighbour in the triad—what the Byzantines addressed as the highest soul, the *nous*. But the idea of the *nous* was substantively redefined in Christian ascetical writing from what it had meant in classical antiquity. It no longer simply connoted intelligence or reason (*logos*)[10]; that form of human ratiocination was seen to reside usually in the upper regions of the middle soul. *Nous* was particularly and distinctively that aspect of graced awareness that constituted a human being most distinctively, and differently from all other created species. For the Byzantine ascetical philosophers, it was the *locus* of the Divine Image in humankind. In its lower range the *nous* would process reflection and thinking, while in its higher ranges it would process transcendental awareness and be the place where the consciousness of the divine image within human consciousness took place and where awareness of God's descent by grace into humanity also registered.

The Byzantine philosophers thus proposed *nous* as the synthetic term covering the dynamic correlation of *logos* and *pneuma*. This reworking of Platonic psychology by the Byzantines into this triadic and flexible view of anthropological constitution, as a system of correlated influences and mediations, gave great dynamism to a new view of human nature and provided a transcendentalism which Plato's theory lacked. If we had more time to explore this, it could be demonstrated that this was none other than an extended patristic theology of the *anastasis* of Christ understood as the

---

10. It has been disastrously translated as *logos* in too many modern versions.

grace of redemption. Plato's theory was seen by the Fathers as defective largely because he had wished to resolve the correlation (*to syntheton*) of soul and body by the intellective dismissal and eventual physical dissolution of the body. By contrast, this elevation of the material form to graced sacramental stature is an important and lasting contribution of Christian Greek philosophy to the importance of the empirical process; it was chiefly made by the fourth- and fifth-century Greek Fathers, who thus stand out as the first wave of significant Byzantine philosophers, although it is a view that is deepened by the sixth- to tenth-century ascetical writers. Empiricism in their hands, however, is not rendered into material reductionism, but into a vision of the human person as transcendental process of transfiguration.[11]

Following from this, the next major achievement of Byzantine patristic philosophy was the doctrine of personhood. In classical Hellenistic thought, following Aristotle's lead, the concept of the person meant *to idion*: something individual, particular, proper—and (accordingly) eccentric. For Aristotle, we may recall, the individual could not serve as the exemplar of true study: it had to be the species, the collective. The individual was the domain of the eccentric, the peripheral. Once again, the Greek Fathers radically changed this widespread view and, by dint of their relentless focus on matters Christological and Trinitarian (in a wide arc of authors taking one another forward, from Origen, through Athanasius and Gregory the Theologian, to Cyril of Alexandria and Maximus the Confessor), they brought forward the notion (and semantic) of personhood (*hypostasis*) to the status of a substantive primary category (and we note that *hypostasis* semantically means "a substantive," that stability which "stands under"). Allying it with their doctrine of the human soul, and attributing the possession of a human soul to the divine Logos made flesh in the God-Man, whose incarnation was thereby a paradigm of the deified regeneration of the human race (*palingennesia, theiosis*), the Greek Fathers were finally able to assert that the Human person was a creature whose transcendence was released from the boundaries of a mortal na-

---

11. The Orthodox conception of redemption as *theiopoiesis*; see further McGuckin, "Deification in Greek Patristic Thought."

ture, to have once more afforded to it the gift of immortality and the possibility of communion with God. The person (first of all, that of the God-Man whose single divine *Hypostasis* both explained and energized the way the incarnation saved the human race) thus became a concept of immense centrality and importance. It thereby started upon a trajectory which would have incalculable results in the history of Christian civilization. Without the major Byzantine Christological contributions, the idea of personhood may well have left Western civilization as untouched by its allure, as it did (for example) in Asian Buddhism, where it remains stalled in the role of an illusory notion (*Maya*).

The Christian Fathers, in short, combined all three available philosophical models of selfhood creatively. To Plato's idea of ascentive epistemology (wisdom as an uplifting way to achieve identity), they added Aristotle's quest for the definitive *ethos* of a nature as well as Plotinos's concept of the awareness of divine potency as the giving of identity's core in the act of communion. They are driven to this synthetic position by their own twin imperatives, the retelling of the tale of human identity through and in the person of Christ, who is the infinite Logos fully inhominated, whose person is thus necessarily substantive because it carries the weight of the second *hypostasis* of the Godhead borne up by the transfiguration of frail flesh. The doctrine of the Incarnation substantivizes, or hypostatizes, the concept of spiritual personhood as the quintessential ethos of the Self, and the ground of communion between Godhead and Manhood. The Christian Fathers, therefore, creatively synthesized classical Greek philosophy with biblical and Christological imperatives, so as to make a distinctly new philosophico-religious statement.

Though the Greek Fathers are the lead in the Evangelical synthesis of this tradition of selfhood, the Christian revisioning of Plato's psychology goes on throughout the life of Christian Byzantium. In the thirteenth and fourteenth centuries, after the Byzantines had recaptured their capital, the Paleologan emperors presided over a last revival of philosophy. In this late flowering, there was a steady stream of significant commentaries produced on Aristotle, Plato, and the Neoplatonic writings of Proclus. Significant examples are the works of Sophonias, Leo Magentenos,

Theodore Metochites, Nikephoros Choumnos, Nikephoras Gregoras, Plethon (the most radical of the Byzantine Neo-Platonists), Gennadios Scholarios, and Bessarion—the last two of whom bring us into the final era of the last days of the empire, which fell to the Ottomans in May 1453. The course of Byzantine philosophy in the time of the Greek Fathers shows a wide range of theologians who were readers of a large and broad library of philosophic texts, including Plato and Aristotle as staples, but also the Stoics, Pythagoreans, and elements of Cynic diatribe. Their greatest achievement, philosophically speaking, was their adaptation of the idea of the self to be a hypostatic force, a sacramental reality capable of bearing the weight of a substantive, and of serving dynamically as a transcendental point of encounter with the divine.

What This May Mean in our Own Time

What might the patristic Byzantine reformulations of the idea of self have to suggest to us today? One of our current societal problems is that this doctrine of selfhood has been profoundly forgotten in a theological curriculum that, since the Enlightenment, has progressively neglected the dominant Christian ascetical tradition, where it is lodged, in favour of apologetic dogmatic theology and pastoral studies. One way forward would be to restore Ascetical Theology to its rightful place as the major stream of thought behind classical Christianity. This would suggest that Christian history is not the record of this or that doctrinal controversy; it is, rather, a sustained essay on soteriology, with personhood as the primary *locus* where the human encounters the divine and is redeemed by the communion. This is obviously not simply an individualistic approach to theology but contains within its core idea of communion the notions of ethical and social transfiguration. Such a view of communion as a fundament of personhood would serve to correct a widespread malaise of narcissism that has crept into secular, non-religious reflection on doctrines of the rights of persons.

This leads us to another great problem, for, having given the idea of the person as substantive to Western civilization, Christian theorists neglected to re-engage with it when, from the early twentieth century onwards, the concept was radically reinterpreted by psychological deconstructionist views. These medical therapeutic approaches, from Freud onwards to our own era, when psychiatry has more or less become a profoundly "chemical" field, argued that the human self is a working model that (often) goes wrong. This brought a reductionist view centre-stage, one that drove out the former transcendentalism from which the idea was first born. Worse than this, perhaps, this modern idea of the self, or the person seeking therapeutic redress, has evolved into the concept of the person with a range of rights over and against other persons. The idea has thus become oppositional, and narcissistically driven; whereas of old, in Christian patristic hands, it was conceived as a *kenotic*[12] gift from the Lord of humility that sought to explain the principle of social communion. In other words, its premises have today been more or less drastically reversed.

The modern human rights agenda, stripped of its transcendentalist basis, however, becomes morally unsustainable. In the Christian system, the self was a critically important and sacred thing, precisely because the person was a representation of the covenant of God with humanity. As we may recall, the key to the Byzantine genius in reinterpreting Aristotle was to redefine empiricism as no longer meaning material reductionism. The close empirical analysis of the self, for them, demonstrated that the essence of achieved human personhood was the observation that the human nature was not a closed *ousia*, such that we were locked into our *genus*. Quite the contrary, it was posed as an ever energized stretching out (*epektasis*) that is the very root of all our brilliant and multifaceted culture yet transcends even that to impress upon our root human consciousness a transcendental force that makes us ask not only what it is that is, but why it is. This "why?" is the dynamic move that at once explains the ascentive thrust of human

---

12. Derived from *kenosis*, self-emptying out (Phil 2:6–11) that motivated the divine Logos to assume humanity as a sacrificial gift of self to liberate enslaved selves. Modern thought of rights of persons has very little left within it of this *phronema* of the Lord of Glory assuming humility as the vehicle of his majesty.

personhood—the strange issue of the qualitative nature of existence[13]—as well as (for Christian philosophy) the quest for that Person who is at once the Why, being the Way, the Truth, and the Life. Byzantine philosophy demands human personhood be seen as essentially *teleotic*. Unlike Aristotle, it goes further in explaining what *Telos* involves, for it knows who *Telos* is.

The human rights agenda, as we have it today in all its fragility, is such a powerfully important force for the good, that surely it is critical that we should not let it sink (as unquestionably it is sinking) because the transcendental imperative it was first designed to express has been muffled and obscured by reductionist simplification. Christians, who once gave this idea to western civilization as a gift from the Fathers, need to be more efficiently heard redrafting those premises we once brought to the making of Europe, the concept of spiritual personhood at the core of moral and societal values.

Bibliography

Cary, Philip. *Augustine's Invention of the Inner Self: The Legacy of a Christian Platonist*. Oxford: Oxford University Press, 2003.

McGuckin, J. A. "Deification in Greek Patristic Thought: The Cappadocian Fathers' Strategic Adaptation of a Tradition." In *Partakers of the Divine Nature: The History and Development of Deification in the Christian Tradition*, edited by Michael J. Christensen and Jeffrey A. Wittung, 95–114. Grand Rapids: Baker Academic, 2008.

———. *The Transfiguration of Christ in Scripture and Tradition*. Studies in the Bible and early Christianity 9. Lewiston, NY: Edwin Mellen, 1986.

---

13. The truly distinctive aspect of the human *genus* on earth: its sense of the moral emerging from the sense of worship.

ENTHRONED UPON THE CHERUBIM: IRENAEUS'S GOSPEL SYMBOLISM AND ITS CHRISTOLOGICAL, BIBLICAL-THEOLOGICAL, AND CODICOLOGICAL RAMIFICATIONS

Charles E. Hill
Reformed Theological Seminary, Orlando, FL, USA

It is not possible that there be more Gospels in number than these, or fewer. By way of illustration, since there are four zones in the world in which we live, and four cardinal winds, and since the Church is spread over the whole earth, and since *the pillar and bulwark* of the Church is the Gospel and the Spirit of life, consequently she has four pillars, blowing imperishability from all sides and giving life [*vivificantes*] to men. From these things it is manifest that the Word, who is Artificer of all things and *is enthroned upon the Cherubim and holds together all things*, and who was manifested to men, gave us the fourfold Gospel, which is held together by the one Spirit. Just as David, when petitioning His [Christ's] coming, said, *You who are enthroned upon the Cherubim, shine forth*. For the Cherubim, too, had four faces (τετραπρόσωπα).[1]

It is safe to say that, despite having launched an array of creative exegetical and artistic traditions, Irenaeus's arguments for the fourfold Gospel, in particular his famous comparison between the four Gospels and the four living creatures of Ezek 1:10 and Rev 4:7, have not won him the universal admiration of modern exegetes.[2] To many, it appears that the second-century bishop made

1. Irenaeus, *Haer.* 3.11.8 (Unger, ACW)
2. Calling forth phrases like "tortured insistence" (Gamble, *New Testament Canon*, 32); "implausible, even as humor" (Funk, "Once and Future New Testament," 543); "early ... but unfortunate" (Swete, *Apocalypse*, 72); "quaintly antique logic" (Patterson, *Gospel of Thomas*, 4); "even in the ancient world ... not the most convincing line of argument" (McDonald, *Biblical Canon*, 291); "curious arguments" (Lienhard, "Canons," 64). The record of scowls could go on.

clever, but perhaps too clever, attempts to find suitable natural and scriptural analogues for his fourfold Gospel. Given the long-term effects, both real and imagined, that have accrued from Irenaeus's deliberations on the fourfold Gospel, the historical/exegetical background for his correlations of the cherubim and the Gospels are surprisingly under-studied. The present essay seeks to expose the exegetical foundations for these correlations, and some of their prehistory in early Christian thought. It then turns to consider more closely Irenaeus's Christological and Biblical-theological elaborations on the living creatures and the Gospels. Finally, it will explore the relationship between these correlations and the arrangements of the books in early Gospel codices.

1. *The Exegetical/Christological Foundation of the Comparison*

1.1 *Christ as the One Seated above the Cherubim*

Irenaeus's comparisons between the four Gospels and the four living creatures in *Haer.* 3.11.8 rest upon a prior exegetical conclusion. That conclusion is that the Old Testament depiction of God as "he who is enthroned above the cherubim" from Ps 80:1 (79:2 LXX) is a depiction not of God the Father, or of God unspecified, but specifically of Christ.[3] It is "the Word," the "Artificer of all things," who is "enthroned upon the Cherubim and holds together all things." So, just as the four cherubim uphold the throne of Christ and give glory to him (*Epid.* 10), so do the four Gospels.

The conception of God as enthroned upon the cherubim had a long history in Israel. It is first met in Exod 25:22, where God told Moses to make the ark with two cherubim: "And there I will meet with you; and from above the mercy seat, from between the two cherubim which are upon the ark of the testimony, I will speak to you about all that I will give you in commandment for the sons of Israel."[4] As the ark of the covenant of Yahweh makes its way to its final resting place in the tabernacle in Jerusalem, it is called

---

3. See also his reference to Ps 99:1 in *Haer.* 4.33.13.
4. Cf. the "cherubim of glory" in Heb 9:5. Images of cherubim were also woven into the curtains of the tabernacle (see Exod 26:31; 36:8; 2 Chr 3:14).

"the ark of the covenant of the LORD of hosts who sits above the cherubim" (1 Sam 4:4; cf. 2 Sam 6:2).

The theme then emerges in the Psalms. Psalm 79:2 LXX begins with the petition "Give ear, O Shepherd of Israel, you who lead Joseph like a flock. You who are enthroned upon the cherubim (ὁ καθήμενος ἐπὶ τῶν χερουβιν), shine forth (ἐμφάνηθι)." As recorded in both 2 Kgs 19:15 and Isa 37:16, King Hezekiah addressed the LORD under this title in prayer: "O LORD, the God of Israel, who art enthroned above the cherubim, Thou art the God, Thou alone, of all the kingdoms of the earth. Thou hast made heaven and earth."

The conception reaches its zenith in the elaborated visions of Ezek 1 and 10.[5] Instead of just two cherubim, we read that Ezekiel beheld "four living creatures," who in Ezek 10 are called cherubim, each of whom had four faces, beside each of whom was a wheel. Above the creatures was the likeness of a throne, "and seated above the likeness of a throne was a likeness with a human appearance" (Ezek 1:26).

The depiction of the LORD as enthroned above the cherubim is established in the praises, prayers, and the architecture of Israel's worship from the Pentateuch through the Prophets. This complex of Old Testament images of the heavenly quartet, we shall now see, had a vibrant presence in the Christian piety of at least three pre-Irenaean authors who hail from or have strong ties to Asia Minor.[6]

1.2 The Epistula Apostolorum

The *Epistula Apostolorum*, an Asian work probably from the first half of the second century,[7] praises Christ as "Power of the heav-

---

5. See also in the additions to Daniel (Dan 3:55 LXX): "Blessed are you who look into the depths, sitting over the cherubim (καθήμενος ἐπὶ χερουβιμ), and to be praised and highly exalted forever."

6. By comparison, Origen seems to know nothing of this exegetical tradition, from his homilies on Ezekiel (see Pearse, ed., *Origen of Alexandria*).

7. On Asia Minor as provenance, see Schmidt and Wajnberg, *Gespräche Jesu*; Hill, "*Epistula Apostolorum*." Francis Watson (*Apostolic Gospel*, 11) affirms the Asianic provenance but dates the work later, to ca. 170, based primarily on a definitive identification of the plague mentioned in *Epistula Apostolorum*

enly Powers, who sits above the Cherubim [and Seraphim][8] at the right hand of the throne of the Father" (*Ep. Apos.* 3:3–4).[9] Here, as in Irenaeus, it is emphatically Christ who sits above the cherubim (Ps 79:2 [98:1 LXX]) at the right hand of the throne of the Father. The title "Power of the heavenly Powers" seems to derive from the refrain in Ps 79:5, 8, 15, 20 LXX, "O Lord, the God of mighty powers" (κύριε ὁ θεὸς τῶν δυνάμεων). The *Epistula Apostolorum*'s expression is also interesting for its wedding of the Christological interpretation of the one seated above the cherubim to the divine summons "sit at my right hand" from Ps 109:1 (110:1 MT), which of course the New Testament takes as spoken to Jesus the Christ.

1.3 *Justin*

Justin, too, is familiar with the exegesis which identifies Christ as the one seated above the cherubim. In *Dial.* 37.2–3, he claims that the divine figure in Ps 98:1 (99:1 MT) is the coming king.

> And in Psalm Ninety-eight the Holy Spirit reprimands you and announces that he whom you refuse to recognize as your king is *the King and Lord of Samuel, Aaron, Moses*, and of every other man. Here are the words of that psalm: *The Lord has reigned, let the peoples be angry. He that sits on the cherubim; let the earth be moved.*[10]

34, 36 as the "Antonine Plague" of 165–170. This is of course possible but, based on a good deal more of the "extant evidence," not quite as probable as an earlier date, just before 150 (see Hill, "*Epistula Apostolorum*"). Not for the first time, Watson (*Apostolic Gospel*, 11n24) has misread an argument and felt free to publish imagined motives. In any case, the Ep. Apos. appears to predate Irenaeus's *Against Heresies*.

8. Most MSS have "and Seraphim," according to Watson (*Apostolic Gospel*, 222), and only MS A omits it. Watson decides for "Cherubim" alone as original because "the pairing of Cherubim and Seraphim appears to be relatively late," even though "'Seraphim and Cherubim' occurs in Origen" (222). The inclusion of Seraphim would signify a reading of Isa. 6, and the comingling of elements from the cherubim vision of Ezek 1 and the seraphim vision of Isa 6 is witnessed already in Rev 4:6–8.

9. The translation of Watson, *Apostolic Gospel*, 45.

10. The translation in Slusser, ed., *Justin Martyr*.

Deeply offended by Justin's exegesis, Trypho then accuses the Christian of blasphemy for claiming that the divine depictions pertain to a crucified man (*Dial*. 38). But for Justin, as for the author of the *Epistula Apostolorum*, the one who sits upon the cherubim is none other than Jesus Christ.

Justin does not directly mention the cherubim of Ezek 1:10 in his extant writings. But he is familiar with the Christological exegesis we are considering, for, in keeping with his own exegesis of Ps 98:1, Justin is convinced that the figure who is in the likeness of a man, above the cherubim in Ezek 1:10, is Jesus. In *Dial*. 126.1, he chides Trypho, "if you had known who he is who at one time is called *angel of great counsel* and *Man* by Ezekiel." The "man" here is clearly the human form "above" the cherubim in Ezek 1:5 LXX ("the likeness of a man was over them" ὁμοίωμα ἀνθρώπου ἐπ' αὐτοῖς) and Ezek 1:26, "and seated above the likeness of a throne was a likeness with the appearance of a man" (καὶ ἐπὶ τοῦ ὁμοιώματος τοῦ θρόνου ὁμοίωμα ὡς εἶδος ἀνθρώπου). For Justin, this is another manifestation of Christ, seated above the cherubim.[11]

1.4 *Melito of Sardis*

The extract known as Fragment 15 is not securely attributable to Melito; a different form of this fragment is transmitted in some Syriac manuscripts under the name of Irenaeus. The close similarities in style and wording to Melito's *Peri Pascha* and verified fragments of his other works, however, weigh strongly in his favor. After surveying the evidence, Stuart Hall decides cautiously for Melito as its author.[12] If this is correct, the Fragment is probably either from Melito's *On the Faith* or his *Extracts* and was written probably a decade or so before Irenaeus's magnum opus. The Fragment is a collection of testimonies to Christ "from the law and the prophets," though it also gathers material from the Gospels. Lines 66 and 67 call Christ

> the Charioteer of the Cherubim,

---

11. This will be further substantiated by Irenaeus's similar exegesis in *Haer*. 4.20.10 as we shall see below.
12. Hall, *Melito of Sardis*, xxxviii.

the chief of the army of angels.[13]

As with the *Epistula Apostolorum*, the reference to the cherubim appears to rely on Ps 79:2 LXX, as the mention of Christ as the chief of the host of angels seems to draw from the psalm's refrain, "O Lord, the God of mighty powers," repeated in vv. 5, 8, 15, 20 LXX (though an allusion to Josh 5:14–15 is possible). The "charioteer" idea, however, while it might possibly be constructed on the basis of Christ simply being seated above the cherubim, or from the "riding" or "flying" mentioned in Ps 17:11[14] (18:10 MT) and 2 Sam 22:11,[15] more likely denotes a dependence on Ezekiel's vision in Ezek 1:15–21, which reports wheels beneath the four living creatures and portrays the throne as a chariot. This Ezekielian image is famously the basis for Jewish Merkabah mysticism, meditation on the heavenly chariot-throne.[16] Christ as "Charioteer of the Cherubim" likely reflects the interplay of multiple Old Testament texts to create a striking and memorable image.

1.5 *Irenaeus*

When Irenaeus, in *Haer*. 3.11.8, then, invokes Christ as the one "enthroned upon the cherubim" and then cites David's petition "You who are enthroned upon the Cherubim, shine forth" just before he gives his analogy of four living creatures and four Gospels, he is not simply dressing up an anxious analogy with serendipitous biblical ornamentation. The movement of thought went the other way. The existing Christological interpretation of the one en-

---

13. Hall's translation; see *Melito of Sardis*, 83n68, which also gives Richard's reconstruction of the Greek: ὁ ἡνίοχος τῶν χερουβίμ, ὁ ἀρχιστράτηγος τῶν ἀγγέλων (Richard, "Témoins grecs").

14. "And he mounted on cherubs and flew: he flew on the wings of winds" (translations of the LXX are from *The Lexham English Septuagint*: καὶ ἐπέβη ἐπὶ χερουβιν καὶ ἐπετάσθη ἐπετάσθη ἐπὶ πτερύγων ἀνέμων).

15. "And he mounted upon the cherubim and flew, and he was seen upon the wings of the wind" (καὶ ἐπεκάθισεν ἐπὶ Χερουβιν καὶ ἐπετάσθη καὶ ὤφθη ἐπὶ πτερύγων ἀνέμου).

16. At Qumran, 4Q385 frag. 4–6; see 1 En 14:8–25; 71:5–11; 2 En 22; see also 3 En ("The vision which Ezekiel saw . . . the gleam of the chariot and four living creatures"); see P. Alexander's excellent introduction, "3 (Hebrew Apocalypse of) Enoch"; Eskola, *Messiah and the Throne*.

throned upon the cherubim became the springboard for comparing the four cherubim to the four Gospels. We can see that the comparison grew from the soil of a well-attested exegetical tradition, known among Christian interpreters in at least Asia Minor and Rome.[17] The connection is explicit in *Haer.* 3.11.8 as Irenaeus introduces the comparison with the four Gospels.[18]

> From these things it is manifest that the Word, who is Artificer of all things and *is enthroned upon the Cherubim and holds together all things*,[19] and who was manifested (φανερωθείς) to men, gave us the fourfold Gospel (τετράμορφον τὸ εὐαγγέλιον), which is held together by the one Spirit. Just as David, when petitioning His [Christ's] coming, said, *You who are enthroned upon the Cherubim, shine forth* (ἐμφάνηθι; Ps. 80:1b [LXX 79:2].[20]

When David implored the enthroned one to "shine forth," he was petitioning the manifestation, the coming, of the Christ. And it is this Christ, the Word, the Artificer[21] of all things, who, after his manifestation, has given us the fourfold Gospel, held together

---

17. The influence of Ezekiel's cherubim throne vision is seen in at least two more places in the writings of Irenaeus. In *Dem.* 10, he refers to the "Powers" of the Word and of Wisdom (i.e., Christ and the Holy Spirit), "which are called Cherubim and Seraphim," likely denoting (as with the *Epistula Apostolorum* and Melito) a dependence on the refrain of Ps 79, and a Christological interpretation of the one who sits above the cherubim. And in *Haer.* 4.20.10 (see below), he refers again to Ezekiel's vision of the cherubim and above them "the appearance of the likeness of the glory of the Lord."

18. *Haer.* 3.11.8 is very fortunately preserved in Greek, the Fr. 11 from Anastasius Sinaita, *Quaestio 144* and the so-called "Grand Notice," a passage copied into several Gospel or catena MSS from the eleventh–sixteenth centuries (see Rousseau and Doutreleau, SC 210, 108), which the Latin by and large translates closely.

19. Cf. Wisd 1:7; Isa 40:22 LXX "It is he that comprehends (ὁ κατέχων) the circle of the earth." Irenaeus's thought here is anticipated by Athenagoras, *Embassy*, 6.3 ("since we cherish that being as God by whose Word all things are made and by whose Spirit all things are held in being") and 13.2 ("upholding all and overseeing all things"). Cf. also Origen, *De princ.* 1.3.5.

20. Irenaeus, *Haer.* 3.11.8 (Unger, ACW) (emphasis original)

21. The word is τεχνίτης, and it had been used in 1.8.1 for the "skillful artist" who created out of precious jewels a beautiful image of a king, which was destroyed by re-arranging the gems into the shape of a dog or a fox.

by the one Spirit. The fourfold Gospel appears to be the Word's ongoing manifestation to men.

We saw above that Justin had pointed Trypho to the one called "Man" in Ezekiel, referring to the one in the form of man in Ezek 1:5, 26. Irenaeus's treatment of this text in *Haer.* 4.20.10 is lengthier and more sophisticated. When Ezekiel beheld "*the likeness of a throne* above them, and on the throne *a likeness as of man's appearance* (Ezek 1:26) . . . he added, *This was the appearance of the likeness of the glory of the Lord*, lest anyone should think that he saw God perfectly in these things" (Ezek 1:28b [2:1 LXX]).[22] What Moses, Elijah, and Ezekiel, "who had all many celestial visions" saw was not God the Father, but "similitudes of the splendor of the Lord, and . . . things to come."

A major reason for Irenaeus's careful avoidance of the thought that Ezekiel saw God (the Father) perfectly is that the Lord said in John's Gospel: "No one has ever seen God; the Only-begotten God, who is in the bosom of the Father, he has made him known" (John 1:18). Irenaeus cited this statement once in *Haer.* 4.20.6 and twice in 4.20.11, along with Exod 3:20, "'But,' he said, 'you cannot see my face; for no one shall see me and live,'" just before and after treating several Old Testament theophanies. He also cited the same Johannine pronouncement in 3.11.6, just before his treatment of the fourfold Gospel in the likeness of the four living creatures in 3.11.8. This declaration functioned as a primary hermeneutical guide for interpreting the Old Testament theophanies in general, and Ezekiel's vision in particular.[23] The same Gospel even provided a pattern for later readers by interpreting Isaiah's vision of the Lord of hosts (Isa 6:1–13) as a vision of Jesus (John 12:41, "Isaiah said this because he saw his glory and spoke about him"), an exegesis followed by Irenaeus.[24] Irenaeus is the only one to state the principle and its Johannine anchor, but it is

---

22. Irenaeus, *Haer.* 4.20.10 (Unger, ACW).

23. "So the Prophets did not see God's very face openly but the economies and mysteries by which man would see God" (Irenaeus, *Haer.* 4.20.10 [Unger, ACW]).

24. Irenaeus, *Haer.* 4.33.11 (Unger, ACW), "Some of them [i.e., the prophets] saw him in glory and beheld his glorious mode of life *at the right of the Father*"; see also 4.20.8.

operative no less in other second-century Christian exegetes like Justin, Melito, and the author of the *Epistula Apostolorum*. These interpreters took John 1:18 to heart and concluded that Old Testament theophanies, even the heavenly visions of God seen by prophets, were revelations of Christ or similitudes of his appearing, given by Christ himself in his capacity as revealer of God.

The point of this section is to show that when Irenaeus in *Haer.* 3.11.8 composed his comparison of the four Gospels to the four cherubim, he was first of all enlarging upon a robust tradition of Christian biblical interpretation that had preceded him. This tradition understood Christ as the divine Person enthroned upon the cherubim in the Psalms of David, numinously present above the ark of the covenant in tabernacle and temple and encountered in Ezekiel's inaugural vision by the river Chebar.

2. *The Four Living Creatures as Images of Christ's Πραγματεία*

What is the symbolism of the cherubim's faces? In Irenaeus's mind the faces do not represent, as Origen would later suggest, the human faculties (Origen, *Hom. Ezek.* 1). Nor do they or their counterparts in Rev 4:6–8 simply represent, as in many modern interpretations, the animate creation, or the fulness or the excellence of the created world.[25] Instead, they depict aspects of the person and work of Christ, as bearing his chariot-throne. It is their Christ-bearing function that makes them fitting subjects of comparison with the four written Gospels.

Irenaeus had introduced the Gospels as a known group of four in *Haer.* 3.1.1. This is a historically oriented section in which he narrates how the church has received the faith and the plan of salvation from those very men through whom the Gospel itself has

---

25. E.g., on Ezekiel, Allen (*Ezekiel 1–19*, 31) says, "As supernatural beings, they are mediators of Yahweh's powerful being. Yet, as his supernatural servants, they also represent the concerted best that each of his orders of animate creation can separately contribute to his glory." On Revelation, Swete says, "The four forms suggest whatever is noblest, strongest, wisest, and swiftest in animate Nature" (*Apocalypse*, 71), which is closely reprised in Ford, *Revelation*, 75: "symbolic of creation and the divine immanence. They are what is noblest (lion), strongest (ox), wisest (man), and swiftness (eagle)."

come down to us, first (in its Scriptural form) from Matthew, then from Mark and Luke, then John. After a lengthy excursus occasioned by his opponents' attacks on these Scriptures in preference to their own "tradition," he comes back to the testimony of the Gospel writers to the "first principles of the Gospel" in 3.9.1. Here beginning with Matthew (3.9.1–3), he then treats Luke (3.10.1–4), then Mark (3.10.5), and then John (3.11.6). In the next section, Irenaeus observes, "the authority of these Gospels is so great that the heretics themselves bear witness to them, and each one of them tries to establish his doctrine with the Gospels as a starting point" (3.11.7).[26] Despite the heretics' protestations, then, proofs drawn from these Gospels are validated even by the heretics themselves. Though Irenaeus has been working with the four Gospels throughout his volumes, to this point he has felt no need to defend the idea that there are four and only four of them. This argument only comes in 3.11.8, and the next section, 3.11.9, discloses the reason why: some of the heretics "destroy the form of the gospel by falsely introducing either more faces to the Gospel than the aforementioned, or fewer."[27] Because of this, Irenaeus has to insist at the beginning of 3.11.8:

> It is not possible that there be more Gospels in number than these, or fewer. By way of illustration, since there are four zones in the world in which we live, and four cardinal winds,[28] and since the Church is spread over the whole earth, and since *the pillar and bulwark* of the Church is the Gospel and the Spirit of life, consequently she has four pillars, blowing imperishability from all sides and giving life [*vivificantes*] to men. From these things it is manifest that the Word, who is Artificer of all things and *is enthroned upon the Cherubim and holds together all things*, and who was manifested to men, gave us the fourfold Gospel, which is held together by the one Spirit. Just as David, when petitioning His [Christ's] coming, said, *You who are enthroned*

---

26. For a convenient chart listing the heretics and their use of the Gospels, see Mutschler, "Irenäus und die Evangelien," 229.

27. As mentioned, Unger's translation in the ACW series italicizes citations. But it missed that Irenaeus is citing John's words in this section (note the "he says"). I have thus italicized them.

28. Cf. Ezek 37:9 and Rev 7:1, which, however, have four angels: κρατοῦντας τοὺς τέσσαρας ἀνέμους τῆς γῆς.

> *upon the Cherubim, shine forth.* For the Cherubim, too, had four faces (τετραπρόσωπα),[29] and their faces are images of the dispensation (εἰκόνες τῆς πραγματείας) of the Son of God.

Irenaeus comes to his analogy between the Gospels and the heavenly beings from the belief that Christ is the one enthroned upon the cherubim—and this ties him directly to Ezekiel, whose prophecy plays a larger role in Irenaeus's thought in this passage than is often appreciated. For instance, Hort noted that Irenaeus's mention here of the "four cardinal winds" and the four pillars "blowing imperishability from all sides and giving life to men" come from reflection on Ezek 37:9, "And he said to me, 'Prophesy to the spirit! Prophesy, son of man, and say to the spirit, "This is what the Lord says; 'Come from the four winds, and blow into these corpses, and they will live (ζησάτοσαν).'"""[30] Just as the spirit in Ezekiel will come from the four winds to breathe life-giving breath on the corpses, so the Spirit now blows imperishability through the four pillars of the Gospel to make people live.

The close similarity of Ezekiel's cherubim to the four living creatures in John's vision in Rev 4:6–8 assured a natural transfer of symbolic significance from the former to the latter. Irenaeus thus immediately slides into John's presentation:

> *For the first one,*[31] he says, *was like a lion,* symbolizing His powerful, sovereign, and kingly nature (τὸ ἔμπρακτον αὐτοῦ καὶ ἡγεμονικὸν καὶ βασιλικὸν χαρακτηρίζον). *The second was like a calf,* symbolizing His ministerial and priestly rank (τὴν ἱερουργικὴν καὶ ἱερατικὴν τάξιν εμφαῖνον). *The third animal had a face like a man,* which manifestly describes His coming as man. *The fourth is like a flying eagle,* manifesting the gift of the Spirit hovering over the Church. (*Haer.* 3.11.8)

Irenaeus is knowingly citing John in the Apocalypse, for he inserts "he says" (φησίν), but he does not identify the source, and his shift from Ezekiel to John is abrupt. These irregularities, T. C.

---

29. Literally, "are four-faced." This is from Ezek 1:6, 10. The "too" means both the Gospel and the cherubim are four-faced (τετράμορφον τὸ εὐαγγέλιον, the four-formed Gospel).

30. Robinson, "Selected Notes," 156.

31. Here, and with the other introductions below, I have added italics to the cited words which Unger has not.

Skeat thought, proved that Irenaeus was somewhat carelessly copying from an intermediary source and had skipped some material. This earlier source, Skeat reasoned, must then have already related the four Gospels to the vision of Ezekiel and to Revelation.[32] But this hardly seems like proof. Because of what we have seen of the Asian Christological exegesis that preceded Irenaeus, we certainly cannot rule out the possibility that the connections between the four Gospels and Ezekiel's four cherubim had been made before him. But it is easier to believe that Irenaeus simply neglected to mention John (whom he had cited and will continue to cite throughout his work) than an otherwise unknown, intermediary source.

Irenaeus's abrupt switch from Ezekiel's vision of the living creatures to John's is more likely because he is anticipating the application he will draw in the next section to the activity of the Son of God in salvation history. This activity, as he perceives it, followed the order of presentation in John's vision of the animals in the Apocalypse.

To be emphasized here is how the Christological interpretation of the one enthroned upon the cherubim led to Christological interpretations of the cherubim themselves. Before he relates the cherubim to the Gospels, Irenaeus first teaches that these figures who support the divine throne illustrate aspects of Christ's πραγματεία, his dealings, his operations, his careful working among mankind. It is, first of all, the cherubim, not the Gospels, that set forth "images of the πραγματεία of the Son of God." Before he reaches the end of 3.11.8, Irenaeus will deliver two more analogies based on the four cherubim: for one of which the order of Revelation is important, for the other the order of Ezekiel.

---

32. Skeat, "Irenaeus and the Four-Gospel Canon," 198. For Skeat, this source was a "defence of the Four-Gospel Canon," and it "must have originated at a date early enough to be used as a source by Irenaeus—say, perhaps, not later that [sic] 170 or thereabouts."

2.1 The Lion. Effectual Working, Leadership, Royal Power: John

> *For the first one*, he says, *was like a lion*, symbolizing His powerful, sovereign, and kingly nature (τὸ ἔμπρακτον αὐτοῦ καὶ ἡγεμονικὸν καὶ βασιλικὸν χαρακτηρίζον) (*Haer.* 3.11.8)

At this point, Irenaeus is still speaking of the visionary depictions of the living beings themselves (not the Gospels). The one in the form of the lion represents the "powerful, sovereign, and kingly nature" of Christ. It is only after briefly noting how each of the four beings symbolizes the workings of the Son of God, that Irenaeus then turns to the Gospels:

> Now, the Gospels harmonize (σύμφωνα/*consonantia*) with these [animals] on which Christ Jesus *is enthroned*. For the Gospel according to John narrates the generation which is from the Father, sovereign, powerful, and glorious (ἡγεμονικὴν αὐτοῦ καὶ πρακτικὴν καὶ ἔνδοξον γενεάν). It runs thus, *In the beginning was the Word, and the Word was with God, and the Word was God*; and *all things were made through Him, and without Him was not anything made*. On this account this Gospel is full of all confidence (παρρησίας/*fiducia*), for such is its characteristic (*persona*) (*Haer.* 3.11.8)

The Gospel symbolism is logically secondary to the symbolic witness each heavenly being itself bears to Christ; nevertheless, the four Gospels positively harmonize with them. It is important to note that the comparison between the living beings and the Gospels is not, for Irenaeus, a first-order referentiality. Later expositors, like Victorinus, will flatly state, "The four animals are the four Gospels (*Comm. Rev.* 4.3) . . . The animal similar to the lion is the Gospel according to John (4.4)," etc.[33] For Victorinus and many others,[34] the Gospels (or the evangelists) are the direct referents of the visionary forms. This is typically assumed to be Irenaeus's meaning as well, but it is not. The four living beings

---

33. Translations of Victorinus's commentary are taken from Weinrich, ed., *Latin Commentaries on Revelation*, 1–22.

34. E.g., Apringius of Beja, *Explanation of the Revelation* 4:7, "*The first living creature was like a lion.* Most of our interpreters say that this signifies the person of Mark, the Evangelist" (see Weinrich, *Latin Commentaries on Revelation*, 41).

and the four Gospels bear witness to the Son of God, and they do so in ways that "harmonize"[35] with one another.

Like the lion-cherub, the Gospel according to John narrates Christ's sovereign, powerful and glorious generation from the Father. Irenaeus's association of the lion with John is, of course, not the one we are most accustomed to. After the time of Jerome, particularly in the West, the dominant paradigm has the lion representing Mark and the eagle John (more on this below). But Irenaeus, who is the first we know of to make the associations, confidently links John to the lion and Mark to the eagle.

This unique "generation" of the Word made flesh, his divine origin, is of course one of the hallmarks of John's Gospel, recognized by every interpreter, and its importance for early Christian theology can hardly be overstated.[36] If divine generation, power, and glory are well symbolized by the lion, then the lion-cherub is indeed "consonant" with the Gospel according to John: "for such is its *persona*."

Unger translates the word *persona* here as "characteristic" (i.e., "for such is its characteristic"). This portion is missing from the Greek of Fragment 11 but Rousseau and Doutreleau's restoration of the word πρόσωπον is surely correct. This is the same word Irenaeus had already used to describe the faces of the cherubim, as τετραπρόσωπα καὶ τὰ πρόσωπα αὐτῶν εἰκόνες τῆς πραγματείας τοῦ Υἱοῦ τοῦ Θεοῦ (lines 183–84).

The (singular) Gospel too is four-faced, for in 3.11.9 he will charge that some heretics "destroy the form of the gospel by falsely introducing either more faces (πρόσωπα) to the Gospel than the aforementioned, or fewer." The repeated reference to "faces" indicates again that the comparison was grounded upon Ezekiel's vision, where each living creature is said to be four-faced. And "face" seems to have an application to each of the written Gospels

---

35. The word is σύμφωνα, which the Latin translator appropriately rendered as *consonantia*. The two foursomes agree or "make the same sound;" they each set forth these truths about the Son of God.

36. For Justin alone, see Hill, *Johannine Corpus*, 316–37; more generally, Wiles, *Spiritual Gospel*; Hill, "Gospel of John."

themselves, as Irenaeus finds the character of each Gospel at its "face," that is, at its beginning.[37]

2.2 *The Ox. His Sacrificial and Sacerdotal Order: Luke*

> The second was like a calf, symbolizing His ministerial and priestly rank (*Haer*. 3.11.8)

Again, the calf or ox (μόσχος) of Rev 4:7 signifies not, in the first place, a Gospel, but *Christ's* sacrificial and sacerdotal activity. It also becomes a fitting symbol for Luke's presentation of Christ in his Gospel. Further down in 3.11.8, Irenaeus explains:

> The Gospel according to Luke, since it has a priestly character (ἱερατικοῦ χαρακτῆρος ὑπάρχον), began (ἤρξατο) with Zacharias the priest as he was offering incense to God. For the fatted calf which would be slaughtered when the younger son would be found was already being prepared.

Again, Irenaeus finds the priestly character of the Gospel according to Luke clearly discernable at its opening (its face), where in the very first episode Luke tells the story of the priest Zechariah, the father of John the Baptist, ministering in the temple. Luke even uses word μόσχος, as Irenaeus says, when, upon the return of the prodigal, the father orders the slaughter of the fatted calf to make a celebratory feast (Luke 15:27, 30). Luke is the only Evangelist to use the word, its only other NT occurrences being in Heb 9:12, 19, where the calf[38] is a sacrificial animal meant for burnt offerings and sin offerings in the Levitical system (Exod 24:6; Lev 16:6).

2.3 *The Man. His Advent as a Human Being: Matthew*

> The third animal had *a face as of a man*, which manifestly describes His coming as man (*Haer*. 3.11.8).

---

37. The connection of the "face" of each Gospel and its beginning is clearly assumed in Victorinus, *Comm. Rev.* 4.4, and made explicit by Jerome in his *Comm. Ezek.* 1.10, "The *face* means the beginning of the Gospels."

38. μόσχος being used interchangeably with ταῦρος in this passage.

Irenaeus sees in Revelation's third living creature a manifest description of the advent of the Word of God as a human being. Further down in 3.11.8, he shows how it also fittingly depicts the character of Matthew's Gospel:

> Matthew narrates His generation inasmuch as He is man (τὴν κατὰ ἄνθρωπον αὐτοῦ γέννησιν ἐξηγεῖται). *The book*, he writes, *of the generation* (γενέσεως) *of Jesus Christ, the son of David, the son of Abraham* [Matt. 1:1]; and again, *the birth* (ἡ γέννησις) *of Christ took place in this way* [Matt. 1:18]. This Gospel, then, belongs to the human form (ἀνθρωπόμορφον) and so throughout the Gospel the humble and meek man is retained.

More than all the other Gospels, Matthew, according to Irenaeus, emphasizes Jesus' humanity, as is seen in the Evangelist's very first words. Irenaeus keenly aligns the human face of the third living creature with Matthew's commencement of his Gospel with the human "generation" (γενέσεως) or genealogy of Jesus and moving right on to an account of his human birth. This forms a nice complement to Irenaeus's description of John as relating Christ's divine and "glorious generation (γενεάν) from the Father." "Anthropomorphic" describes Matthew's entire Gospel, for "throughout the Gospel the humble and meek man is retained."

2.4 *The Flying Eagle. The Gift of the Spirit*

> *The fourth is like a flying eagle*, manifesting (σαφηνίζον) the gift of the Spirit hovering over the Church (*Haer.* 3.11.8)

At first sight, the depiction of the fourth living creature as a flying eagle seems to have to do not with the Son of God per se but with the Spirit. But by stressing the Spirit as "gift,"[39] Irenaeus already hints that he has in mind a connection to Christ's work in "baptizing with the Holy Spirit" (Luke 3:16), and in "pouring out this which you see and hear" (Acts 2:33). This in fact becomes plain later in the chapter when, expanding on the activity of the Lord, he says, "Finally, having become man for us, He sent the gift of

---

39. Earlier in 3.11.8, the four-formed Gospel itself is Christ's gift, held together by the one Spirit.

the heavenly Spirit upon the entire earth, covering us with His pinions."

For Irenaeus, the flying eagle, symbolizing "the gift of the Spirit hovering over the Church," fittingly applies to Mark's Gospel because

> Mark began (τὴν ἀρχὴν ἐποιήσατο) with the prophetical Spirit which came down to men from on high. *The beginning* (Ἀρχὴ), he says, *of the Gospel... as it is written in Isaias the prophet*, pointing out the winged image [i.e., the eagle] of the Gospel (τὴν πτερωτικὴν εἰκόνα τοῦ εὐαγγελίου δεικνύων). For this reason he made a compendious and cursory (σύντομον καὶ παρατρέχουσαν) announcement [of the Gospel], for it has a prophetic character[40] (*Haer.* 3.11.8).

Note it is not simply the Spirit but "the prophetical Spirit" who comes down from on high. The flying eagle fittingly depicts Mark's Gospel, for he begins with the prophetical Spirit speaking through Isaiah. Further, Irenaeus describes "the prophetic character" of writing as being "concise and cursory (σύντομον καὶ παρατρέχουσαν),"[41] and this, he says, is also Mark's.

These early observations on Mark's style are noteworthy and perceptive and have even extracted some praise from scholars. In a letter to B. W. Bacon dated April 10, 1919, James Hardy Ropes, then Hollis Professor of Divinity at Harvard, wrote

> The two words σύντομον and παρατρέχουσαν admirably characterize Mark and are also very appropriate to the incisive brevity and habit of touching on salient points which are commonly found (although the former not always) in prophecy. Of course, the actual *use* of these two methods by Mark and by the prophets seems to us to show striking differences, but nevertheless the remark of Irenaeus is ingenious and not without real insight and sound observation.[42]

---

40. Better, "For this is the prophetic character" (προφητικὸς γὰρ ὁ χαρακτὴρ οὗτος). Irenaeus is asserting that these qualities are typical of the prophetic style.

41. "παρατρέχουσαν] rapid, as contrasted with dwelling on a matter" (see Robinson, "Selected Notes," 156).

42. These comments are taken from handwritten excerpts Ropes made from the letter, which I discovered in a copy of Stieren's edition of Irenaeus (vol. I), which once belonged to Ropes. This volume was first owned by Ezra Abbot

Irenaeus has already drawn fruitful analogies between the four living creatures, the work of Christ, and the character of each Gospel. In his correlations we can see the now familiar threefold office of the incarnate, *human* Christ: *prophet*, *priest*, and *king*.[43] But Irenaeus sees more benefit flowing from the visions of the four living creatures, and this surplus treats us to some of his rich biblical theology.

3. The Gospels and Biblical Theology

In the last two portions of *Haer*. 3.11.8, Irenaeus offers two more biblical-theological lessons taught by the four cherubim that uphold the heavenly throne. The first is an expansion on the "activity" (πραγματεία) of the Lord in his dealings with mankind which he had mentioned earlier as symbolized by the four living creatures.

3.1 *The Activity the Lord in Redemptive History*

The sequence of this messianic activity is significant, for we see that its stages play out historically in the order in which the living creatures are mentioned, not in Ezekiel but in Revelation. This, again, is probably why Irenaeus chose to use Revelation's descriptions in the immediately preceding section.

> Now the Word of God Himself used to speak (προσωμίλει), in virtue of His divinity and glory, with the patriarchs[44] who lived before Moses' time. And those who lived under the Law, He used to assign a

---

Jr. and was then purchased by the Harvard Divinity School in 1884. It was subsequently obtained by someone with the initials J. H. I. in March of 1888, from whose legacy it passed into the hands of Ropes in 1902. It is now held in the Roger Nicole Collection at Reformed Theological Seminary in Orlando, having been acquired by Professor Nicole at an unknown time. The handwriting on the note matches the inscription by Ropes at the front of the volume (emphasis original).

43. See Unger, ACW, Book 3 (150n45).

44. On Christ speaking to Abraham and Abraham rejoicing to see Christ's day, see *Haer*. 4.5.3–5; 4.7.1–4

priestly and ministerial function.⁴⁵ Finally, having become man for us, he sent the gift of the heavenly Spirit upon the entire earth, covering us with His pinions. Therefore, such as was the economy (πραγματεία/*dispositio*) of the Son of God, such also was the form (ἡ μορφή) of the living beings; and such as was the form of the living beings, such was also the character (ὁ χαρακτήρ) of the Gospel. And (καί) as the living creatures are fourfold (τετράμορφα), so also the Gospel is fourfold (τετράμορφον); and fourfold also is the Lord's economy (πραγματεία/*dispositio*) (*Haer.* 3.11.8)

Irenaeus concludes with a three-way analogy, and really, a double three-way analogy. It is not simply that the activity of the Lord, the living creatures, and the Gospels are all *fourfold*,⁴⁶ an analogy which Irenaeus mentions second. He begins with another analogy: "such as was the economy (πραγματεία)⁴⁷ of the Son of God, such also was the form (ἡ μορφή) of the living beings; and such as was the form of the living beings, such was also the character (ὁ χαρακτήρ) of the Gospel." The πραγματεία of the Lord is what is paramount, and this πραγματεία is symbolized both by the *visual form* of the heavenly beings (lion, ox, man, and eagle) and by the corresponding *character* of the fourfold Gospel. This particular three-way analogy, as already mentioned, plays upon on the presentation in Rev 4:7, for the epochs of the Lord's activity symbolized unfolded in the same sequence as the four living creatures are presented in Rev 4.7: by his divinity and glory with the patriarchs; his priestly and ministerial order under the law; his incarnation for us; and his giving of the heavenly Spirit to superintend the church. Each is portrayed by the creatures and by the character of the Gospels.

---

45. τάξιν in the Greek fragment, but Latin *actum*, standing for a presumed πρᾶξιν. Unger decides for the latter ("function" above), but Robinson ("Selected Notes," 156) finds that a previous occurrence of τάξιν was rendered correctly as *ordinatio* by the Latin translator. Thus, it is likely that the translation *actum* here was based on a misreading or a corrupted text.

46. Watson, *Gospel Writing*, 509, who writes, "the four heavenly creatures as a group provide Irenaeus with exactly what he needs, a vivid and memorable image of fourfoldness."

47. See Briggman, "Re-evaluating Angelomorphism," 589, who suggests "that πραγματεία refers to aspects of, or moments in, the economy of the Son."

But Irenaeus has not yet finished his analogies. The Ezekielian order has still to yield its fruits.

3.2 *The Four Universal Covenants, and Gospel Order*

> And for this reason four principal (καθολικαί) covenants were given to the human race (*Haer.* 3.11.8)

Irenaeus then lists those four universal covenants, though here there is a problem in the transmission of the text. The surviving form of the Greek fragment names covenants under Noah, Abraham, Moses, and "of the Gospel through our Lord Jesus Christ," but this appears to be corrupt. Most editors and translators seem to believe (and I agree) that the Latin preserves the original better here,[48] and it has covenants with Adam, Noah, Moses, and the new covenant. Since Irenaeus qualifies these covenants as καθολικαί,[49] Adam[50] seems perhaps more likely than Abraham. Also suspect about the Greek version is that it gives signs for the first two covenants (rainbow; circumcision), but not for the last two, and it lacks the very Irenaean flourish at the end (the last clause in the citation below). Unger's translation (using the Latin identifications) is as follows.

> And for this reason four principal covenants were given to the human race: the first, of (ἐπί) Adam before the deluge; the second, of (ἐπί) Noe after the deluge; the third, the law (ἡ νομοθεσία) under (ἐπί) Moses; and the fourth, which renews man and recapitulates in itself all

---

48. See the reasons given in SC 210.286. The *ANF*, Unger (ACW), and the French of SC 211 all follow the Latin. Rousseau, however, thought we should retain the order of the Greek (SC 211.494–495, which refers to SC 406, "Appendice V: Les quatre alliances," 385–88).

49. *Generi* in the Latin. Cf. the reference to the Noahic covenant in *Dem.* 22, "But after the flood God established a covenant for the whole world, and for all living beasts, and for men."

50. For more of Irenaeus's reflections on the role of Adam in his transgression, and as the object of redemption by Christ, see *Haer.* 3.23.1–8; *Dem.* 15–17.

things,[51] that is, which through the Gospel raises up and bears men on its wings to the heavenly kingdom. (*Haer.* 3.11.8)

Immediately we see that the four principle or universal covenants do not follow the same *sequence* as Revelation. The fourth covenant (the same in Greek and Latin) is certainly the eagle—bearing mankind on its wings into the heavenly kingdom and picking up on the "winged" aspect of the Gospel. For Irenaeus, this would be Mark. The third, the giving of the law under Moses (also the same in both versions) would be the sacerdotal ox, meaning Luke. The second, as Noah introduces the patriarchal period which Irenaeus previously identified as the time of Christ interacting in a royal and divine manner, like the lion, would be John. And, that the first covenant, under Adam the first man, should correspond to the human face (Matthew), makes excellent sense.[52]

What this means is that, for Irenaeus, while the Son's fourfold activity in redemptive history flowed in the order of John's four living creatures, the four principal, divine covenants came in the order of the four faces of the cherubim in Ezek 1:10: man, lion, ox, and eagle.[53]

4. *Ezekiel's Cherubim and Gospel Sequencing*

Into his discussion of the number and character of the fourfold Gospel Irenaeus has profitably incorporated John's vision of the four living creatures in the Apocalypse, finding biblical-theological significance in John's sequencing. But the more primary, foundational role of Ezekiel, along with Ps 79 and the other thematical-

---

51. Shades of Eph 1:10 here, "as a plan for the fullness of time, to unite (ἀνακεφαλαιώσασθαι) all things in him, things in heaven and things on earth."

52. Even the Greek order would seem to require the same identifications. In this case, Abraham would most likely represent the patriarchs and thus be matched with the lion (John), leaving Noah to be represented by the man (Matthew), perhaps because the entire human race had a new beginning in Noah.

53. Irenaeus elsewhere links the succession of covenants in Scripture to God's gradual perfecting of mankind: "He was manifested to men just as God willed, in order that by believing in him they might always make progress and might through the covenants make progress toward the perfection of salvation" (4.9.3); for more on man's progress, see 4.38.

ly consonant passages, is clear, both for the exegetical tradition that preceded Irenaeus, and for Irenaeus himself as he composed the analogies with the Gospels.

Now, the order in which the cherubim's faces are mentioned in Ezek 1:10 (man, lion, ox, eagle) using Irenaeus's identifications, would yield the Gospel order Matthew, John, Luke, and Mark. And this, as Skeat recognized in a well-known 1992 article,[54] turns out to be the so-called Western order of the Gospels. Skeat could also have noted a corollary of this, that is, if one rejects Irenaeus's correlations in favor of those later articulated by Jerome, the present canonical order, too, can be found in the order of the faces in Ezekiel: the man is Matthew, the lion is Mark, the ox is Luke, and the eagle is John. Both orders, in other words, can be derived from Ezekiel's vision.

These observations might be enough to make one wonder if it is possible that the codicological arrangement of the Gospels was in fact founded in some way upon, or ever justified by, the early Christian exegesis of the four living creatures of Ezekiel—or vice versa. Whenever it was that the four Gospels began to be copied, sewn together, and used in single codices, how did the creator(s) decide the order in which they would be placed? Hengel observes that four books in a collection have twenty-four possibilities of sequence.[55] Metzger finds only nine different sequences actually attested among literary and manuscript witnesses, most of them quite minimally.[56] The present canonical order dominates the tradition; only the Western order rivals it, and only in the early period.

The simplest and likeliest explanation for the origin of the present canonical order, Matthew, Mark, Luke, and John, is that it was based on a perceived chronology of their publication.[57] The

---

54. Skeat, "Irenaeus and the Four-Gospel Canon," 197–98, citing also Zahn, *Geschichte des neutestamentlichen Kanons*, 2:370–71.
55. Hengel, "Four Gospels," 17.
56. Metzger, *Canon*, 296–97.
57. Clement of Alexandria was heir to a variant tradition which held that the Gospels with the genealogies were first, and that John was written last, giving the order Matthew, Luke (or Luke, Matthew), Mark, John (Eusebius, *Hist. eccl.* 6.14.5–7).

early literary witnesses who mention the four Gospels in this order—the Muratorian Fragment;[58] Irenaeus in *Haer.* 3.1.1 (though, strictly speaking, he does not say that Mark was issued before Luke) and Origen in his *Comm. Matt.*[59] present them in what is *ostensibly* the order of their historical appearance.[60] The first material witnesses to the Gospels in this order, however, oddly enough, do not come until the fourth century in the pandect codices Vaticanus (B 03) and Sinaiticus (א 01), followed in the fifth century by Alexandrinus (A 02), and then nearly the entire Greek tradition thereafter. But partial evidence for this order may be claimed from P75 (most likely third-century), which holds Luke and John, in that order.[61]

The usual explanation for the origin of the Western order is given by Bruce Metzger: "This order seems to have arisen from a

---

58. Metzger, *Canon*, 296, believed the MF to be the first witness to this order. In my view, the Fragment is probably just later than Irenaeus and is quite possibly aware of Irenaeus's treatment in *Haer.* 3.1.1. The most recent critical edition is that of Rothschild, *Muratorian Fragment. Text*, who, however, takes a very different view of the dating of the MF.

59. Origen (Eusebius, *Hist. eccl.* 6.25.4–5) also quite possibly familiar with Irenaeus's presentation in *Haer.* 3.1.1, writes, "as having learnt by tradition concerning the four Gospels, which alone are unquestionable in the Church of God under heaven, that first was written that according to Matthew, who was once a tax-collector but afterwards an apostle of Jesus Christ, who published it for those who from Judaism came to believe, composed as it was in the Hebrew language. Secondly, that according to Mark, who wrote it in accordance with Peter's instructions, whom also Peter acknowledged as his son in the catholic epistle, speaking in these terms: 'She that is in Babylon, elect together with you, saluteth you; and so doth Mark my son.' And thirdly, that according to Luke, who wrote, for those who from the Gentiles [came to believe], the Gospel that was praised by Paul. After them all, that according to John."

60. Hengel ("Four Gospels," 18) explains the ultimate demise of the Western order: "The 'historical' order was stronger because it was older."

61. Some have thought that P75 would have had a companion volume with Matthew and Mark (Hengel, "Four Gospels," 17). Skeat proposed that P75 "is in fact the second half of a four-Gospel codex, since it consisted, when complete, of a single-quire codex of 72 leaves . . . If then P 75 was originally a four-Gospel codex, it must have consisted of two single-quire codices sewn together, the first containing Matthew and Mark, the second Luke and John;" after noting the papyrus's likely date in the early third century, Skeat remarked, "This, of course, must also have had ancestors" ("Origin," 80–81).

desire to give the two apostles a leading place. As for the two who were held to be associated with apostles, the greater length of Luke's Gospel takes precedence over Mark's Gospel."[62] There might be thought to be some basis for this when Tertullian in his treatise against Marcion (*Adv. Marc.* 4.2) chooses to treat the Gospels written by apostles first, before those written by their associates. But Tertullian's order of treatment was chosen for apologetic reasons, and it is actually John, Matthew, Luke, Mark. If Metzger's explanation is valid, then, it really must involve two principles: apostles first, and, with each pair, the longest Gospel first.

The appellation "Western" appears to have arisen from the fact that, while it now constitutes only a small minority of the Greek tradition, it is the order of the majority of Old Latin Gospel MSS (VL 5, VL 10, etc.).[63] And yet this order is apparently also represented in P45, the earliest surviving Greek copy of all four Gospels (plus Acts) in one codex, from the third century.[64] It is also found in two important fifth-century Greek manuscripts, Codex Bezae (D 05, a Greek/Latin diglot) and Codex Washingtoniensis (W 032).[65] And since the Old Latin manuscripts all seem to derive

---

62. Metzger, *Canon*, 296–97. See also Saydon, "Order," 191.

63. Houghton, *Latin New Testament*, 12. There are exceptions, however. Codex Bobiensis (VL 1), the oldest Latin Gospel book now extant (fourth century), has the peculiar order John, Luke, Mark, Matthew (*Latin New Testament*, 22). Another unusual order is present in the list added to Codex Claromontanus of the Pauline epistles (VL 75), which gives the order Matthew, John, Mark, Luke (*Latin New Testament*, 27).

64. On P45 having the Western order, see Skeat and McGing, "Notes," 21, and Skeat, "Codicological Analysis," 141–57 (esp. 146–47).

65. See also Patton, "Greek Catenae." Besides P45, D 05, and W 032, three more Greek majuscules, X 033 (catena), 055 (catena), and 073+084 exhibit this order, "four from the third to the sixth century and two from a later period" (Patton, "Greek Catenae," 117). There are no Greek minuscule MSS with the Western order (correcting the contrary claim of Metzger, *Canon*, 296), but Patton has recently identified five ninth-to-twelfth-century catena manuscripts in minuscule script, with abbreviated Biblical text, with this order. He does not believe, however, that the seven catena MSS adopted this order because the catenist used a Western order exemplar. This order is also represented in a work known as the *Speculum* or *Liber de diuinis scripturis* (PS-AU spe), falsely attributed to Augustine, compiled in Italy around 400 (Houghton, *Latin New Testament*, 39).

from "a single common original" copy,[66] this early copy, with little doubt, must have come from a particular Greek archetype which had the Gospels in the Western order.

Irenaeus's identifications of the lion with John and the eagle with Mark are followed in later Greek expositions of Revelation, in particular, in Victorinus of Pettau's third-century Latin *Commentary on Revelation*[67] and in the influential Greek commentary of Andrew of Caesarea in Cappadocia in the early seventh century.[68] But it never gained universal acceptance. Augustine, for instance, in his *Harmony of the Gospels* (written ca. 400) first gives the customary, historical order of the Gospels' appearance (Matthew, Mark, Luke, John; *Cons*. 1.2.3), but when he comes to relate them to the living creatures of Revelation, he rejects what amounts to Irenaeus's identifications (he does not mention Jerome's), saying that it looks only to the books' beginnings, not to their wholes. He agrees rather with those "who have taken the lion to point to Matthew, the man to Mark, the calf to Luke, and the eagle to John" (*Cons*. 1.6.9). Augustine's familiarity with at least some aspect of the Ezekielian background is signified almost incidentally when in *Cons*. 1.7.10 he calls the Gospels "those sacred chariots of the Lord . . . in which He is borne throughout the earth and brings the peoples under His easy yoke and His light burden."[69] Augustine's correlations were followed by Bede in his *Exposition of the Apocalypse*.[70]

It is Jerome's correlations, and his justifications of them, that eventually won the day in the West, though this took some time. The first occurrence of these correlations in Jerome's writings comes in his treatise against Jovinian 1.26, written in 393. While

---

66. Houghton, *Latin New Testament*, 12.
67. Victorinus's own edition survives in three MSS found in the Vatican library, the main one being Ottobonian 3288B (fifteenth century); see Bruce, "Earliest Latin Commentary," 355. An English translation of Victorinus's original may be found in Weinrich, *Latin Commentaries*, 1–22. *ANF* (vol. 7) gives Jerome's revised edition.
68. For an English translation see Constantinou, *Guiding to a Blessed End*.
69. So too, Jerome's "team of four" *Ep*. 53.8, on which, see below.
70. For an English translation, see Weinrich, *Latin Commentaries*, 110–95.

expounding the virtues of John, the virgin apostle, he observes that John's Gospel

> is widely different from the rest. Matthew as though he were writing of a man begins thus: "The book of the Generation of Jesus Christ, the son of David, the son of Abraham:" Luke begins with the priesthood of Zacharias; Mark with a prophecy of the prophets Malachi and Isaiah. The first has the face of a man, on account of the genealogical table; the second, the face of a calf, on account of the priesthood; the third, the face of a lion, on account of the voice of one crying in the desert, "Prepare ye the way of the Lord, make His paths straight." But John like an eagle soars aloft, and reaches the Father Himself, and says, "In the beginning was the Word, and the Word was with God, and the Word was God. The same was in the beginning with God," and so on. The virgin writer expounded mysteries which the married could not . . .[71]

Jerome keeps to Irenaeus's practice of reading the character of the Gospels from the way they begin, and cites the very same portions of each Gospel, at or near their beginnings, that Irenaeus had cited as proof for the earlier identifications. But Jerome shows no hesitation at all in changing the lion from Mark to John, and the eagle from John to Mark. Even though his order of presentation here (Matthew, Luke, Mark, John) is neither that of Ezekiel nor that of Revelation, by mentioning the faces of each creature he shows the preeminent influence of Ezekiel.

Jerome's reliance upon Ezekiel is even more apparent in his *Ep.* 53.8 to Paulinus of Nola written the next year (394). Here his introduction to the four Gospels is purely Ezekielian, comparing them to Ezekiel's cherubim with a medley of allusions to Ezek 1:7–20:

> Matthew, Mark, Luke, and John are the Lord's team of four, the true cherubim or store of knowledge. With them the whole body is full of eyes [Ezek. 1:18],[72] they glitter as sparks [Ezek. 1:7], they run and return like lightning [Ezek. 1:14], their feet are straight feet [Ezek. 1:7], and lifted up, their backs also are winged, ready to fly in all directions [Ezek. 1:17]. They hold together each by each and are interwoven one

---

71. W. H. Freemantle's translation from *NPNF*² 6:366.
72. This feature has a parallel in Rev 4:6, 8.

with another [Ezek. 1:9]: like wheels they roll along and go whithersoever the breath of the Holy Spirit wafts them [Ezek. 1:12].[73]

Though he does not expressly say *which* Gospels are represented by *which* faces, his order of presentation is that of Ezekiel's vision, not of John's as Irenaeus had done. Here the metaphor probably aimed at but never verbally completed in Irenaeus is filled out: the Gospels *are* the true cherubim, "the Lord's team of four." As we saw above, only a few years later Augustine would extend the metaphor even further, calling the four Gospels "those sacred chariots of the Lord . . . in which He is borne throughout the earth and brings the peoples under His easy yoke and His light burden."

In the preface to his *Commentary on Matthew* of 398,[74] while clearly influenced by Irenaeus's presentation in *Haer.* 3.1.1, Jerome again specifically centers on Ezekiel and his description:[75]

> The book of Ezekiel also proves that these four Gospels had been predicted much earlier . . . The first face of a man signifies Matthew, who began his narrative as though about a man: "The book of the generation of Jesus Christ the son of David, the son of Abraham." The second [face signifies] Mark in whom the voice of a lion roaring in the wilderness is heard: "A voice of one shouting in the desert: Prepare the way of the Lord, make his paths straight," The third [is the face] of the calf which prefigures (*praefigurat*) that the evangelist Luke began with Zachariah the priest. The fourth [face signifies] John the evangelist who, having taken up eagle's wings and hastening towards higher matters, discusses the Word of God.

Later in the same preface he turns to Revelation as a secondary witness:

> This also explains the words found in the Apocalypse of John . . . and the four living creatures full of eyes. Then it says: "The first living creature was like a lion and the second was like a calf and the third was like a man and the fourth was like a flying eagle." And a little bit later it says: "They were full of eyes and never ceased day and night . . ."

---

73. Freemantle's translation, *NPNF*² 6:101.
74. In four books, hastily written in two weeks in March of 398 to provide Eusebius of Cremona with reading material for traveling! (Kelly, *Jerome*, 222).
75. Citations of the *Comm. Matt.* are from Scheck, *St. Jerome*, 55–56. The Latin is from CCSL 77.3–4.

> By all of these things it is plainly shown that only the four Gospels ought to be received, and all the lamentations of the Apocrypha should be sung by heretics, who, in fact, are dead, rather than by living members of the Church.

In this brief look at the Apocalypse, Jerome does not repeat his individual Gospel-living creatures identifications, but in his revision of Victorinus's *Commentary on the Apocalypse* produced earlier that same year (398),[76] he forges the identity realignments explicitly. Victorinus had followed Irenaeus's correlations,[77] and Jerome, while he kept virtually all Victorinus wrote about Matthew and Luke, boldly changed the lion to Mark and the eagle to John: "Mark, in whom is heard the voice of the lion roaring in the desert . . . John the evangelist, like to an eagle hastening on uplifted wings to greater heights, argues about the Word of God."

One thing that stands out in Jerome's treatments of the subject is the prominence of Ezekiel over Revelation. This is in keeping with the earlier tradition prior to Irenaeus, and with Irenaeus as well, despite his use of Revelation when he makes the Gospel-cherub correlations and his use of Revelation's order for the πραγματεία of the Son of God.

---

76. Jerome had read Victorinus's *Comm. Matt.* by at least 388 (see the preface to his translation of Origen's *Hom. Luke* to Paula and Eustochium); he also wrote about Victorinus in his *Vir. ill.* (392–393). His revised edition of Victorinus's *Comm. Rev.* appeared in 398 and is represented in seven MSS of the twelfth through fifteenth centuries (Bruce, "Earliest Latin Commentary," 354).

77. Victorinus then expanded these associations with another set of Christological comparisons: Christ was "proclaimed as a lion and a lion's whelp" (Gen 49:9); he became man for the salvation of humanity; he offered himself as a sacrifice to God for us, and so is called a calf, and having conquered death, he ascended to heaven "and held out his wings to cover his people," and so "he is called an eagle in flight. "And although there are four proclamations, yet there is really but one proclamation, because it proceeds from one mouth, just as the river in paradise was from one source yet was separated into four streams" (*Comm. Rev.* 4.4). The four streams flowing out of Eden had already by this time became a common metaphor for the four Gospels. Hippolytus (*Comm. Dan.* 1.17) writes, "Christ, himself being the river, is preached in the whole world through the fourfold Gospel"; Cyprian, in *Ep.* 73.10.3 (in 256), says, "and those trees she [i.e., the Church] waters by means of four rivers—that is, by the four Gospels."

Credit for realigning the lion with Mark and the eagle with John is usually given to Jerome. Watson suggests, however, that Jerome may have been influenced by Epiphanius, *On Weights and Measures* 35,[78] which was written in 392,[79] the year before Jerome's first recorded mention of it in his work against Jovinian. Epiphanius is treating the four measures (*xestai*) that he says were contained in the golden jar (*stamnos*) that held the manna (Exod 16:33), and lays out a series of other "fours." This series includes the "four spiritual creatures which were composed of four faces, which typify the coming of the Messiah." Connecting the creatures to "the coming of the Messiah" may seem reminiscent of Irenaeus's πραγματεία of the Son of God, and Epiphanius certainly had used Irenaeus for his earlier work, the *Panarion* (written in 374–377). But Epiphanius's exposition of the faces is in every case quite different from his predecessor's. Epiphanius mentions the "four faces," which comes from Ezekiel, and, like Jerome and unlike Irenaeus, he treats the spiritual creatures in Ezekiel's order (man, lion, ox, eagle), not John's. In fact, Epiphanius's treatment in *Mens.* seems to owe nothing to Revelation. This order, with the new identifications, results in the now traditional sequence of the Gospels.

> One had the face of a man, because the Messiah was born a man in Bethlehem, as Matthew teaches [Matt 2:1–12]. One had the face of a lion, as Mark proclaims him coming up from the Jordan, a lion king, as also somewhere it is written: "the Lord has come up as a lion from the Jordan" [cf. Jer 27:44 LXX; 49:19/50:44 MT]. One had the face of an ox, as Luke proclaims—not he alone, but also the other Evangelists—him who, at the appointed time of the ninth hour [Luke 23:44], like an ox in behalf of the world was offered up on the cross. One had the face of an eagle, as John proclaims the Word who came from heaven and was made flesh [John 1:14] and flew to heaven like an eagle after the resurrection with the Godhead.[80]

Epiphanius's exposition is so different from that of Irenaeus as to suggest that the former is completely independent of the latter. He

---

78. Watson, *Gospel Writing*, 571n46.
79. Dean, ed., *Epiphanius' Treatise*, 2.
80. *Mens.* 35 (Sect. 64d–65a; Dean, ed., *Epiphanius' Treatise*, 52).

uses none of Irenaeus's Scriptural proofs for the identifications but puts out entirely new ones. Could Epiphanius be witness to an older tradition which associated the four Gospels with the four faces of Ezekiel's cherubim?

Jerome knew and greatly respected Epiphanius,[81] but it is not at all obvious that when he wrote against Jovinian he was aware of his elder colleague's exposition in *Mens*. Jerome does not rely on Epiphanius's arguments or his Scriptural proofs but instead uses the very proofs Irenaeus had provided, only switching two of the identities.

The groundwork for the switch had been laid, however, in 384, eight years before Epiphanius even wrote *Mens.*, when Jerome issued his new Latin edition of the Gospels. For this new edition, Jerome's "most obvious innovation," according to Hugh Houghton,[82] was to change the Old Latin order of the Gospels in the codices. In the preface to his revision, he tells bishop Damasus that the Gospels "are to be taken in the following order, Matthew, Mark, Luke, John, as they have been revised by a comparison of the Greek manuscripts. Only early ones have been used."[83] Apparently, this is the sequence of the Gospels Jerome found in the Greek exemplars he used in Rome while working on his translation, though at least one Greek manuscript Jerome used had the Eusebian apparatus, and therefore, could not have been especially "early." Jeremiah Coogan suggests that Jerome's adoption of the new-old order might perhaps have been "to facilitate use of Eusebius's system."[84] What is interesting for our purposes is that the codicological switch from the Old Latin "Western" order to the "Old Greek/New Vulgate" order took place *first*, years before either Jerome or Epiphanius is on record with their (revised) Gospel-cherubim collations. It would thus appear that the change of

---

81. Jerome, acting probably as interpreter and personal advisor, had accompanied the man he calls "Papa Epiphanius" and Paulinus of Antioch in the summer of 382 on a trip to Rome from the east. The two bishops left the city in the spring of 383 but Jerome remained and was soon tasked by Pope Damasus with translating the Gospels (see Kelly, *Jerome*, 80–90).
82. Houghton, *Latin New Testament*, 32.
83. Freemantle's translation (*NPNF*[2] 6:488).
84. Coogan, *Eusebius the Evangelist*, 126.

the lion to Mark and the eagle to John became necessary, at least for Jerome,[85] once he had restored the order of the Old Latin Gospels to that of the older Greek codices he used. And it suggests that the swapping of identities was determined more by antiquarian, codicological interests (and perhaps by a perception of the historical order of writing) than by a deep conviction about how the faces of the cherubim best matched the characters of the particular Gospels.

But this may not completely settle the matter of origins. Could the old, historical order represented in Jerome's time-worn Greek codices itself have been influenced by Ezekiel's vision? When he came to articulate the Gospels' associations with the heavenly beings, Jerome grounded them, just as Epiphanius did, on Ezekiel's vision (rather than on John's). Ezekiel's vision is foundational for both writers. The consistent presence of Ezekiel, passing through Irenaeus to the earlier second-century writers we considered earlier, suggests the possibility that when copyists began to bind the four together in the now traditional sequence, they might have been influenced not simply by a perceived literary history (which, as Clement of Alexandria's tradition attests, was not quite unanimous), but by an inspired, heavenly vision. But how early can we reasonably believe the four Gospels were being put together in physical codices?

---

85. As for Epiphanius, as a native of Palestine, educated in Egypt, and ministering in the East, he is less likely to have been as influenced by Jerome's new Latin Gospel copies as by Greek codices themselves. Epiphanius may simply have followed the order of Greek codices he knew. Epiphanius too had long used a four-Gospel codex, or codices, with the Eusebian apparatus. In his *Ancoratus* 50.6, written in 374, he says there are 1,162 κεφάλαια in the four Gospels; this presupposes his use of four-Gospel codices equipped with the Eusebian canons, as 1,162 is the total of all the Ammonian Sections of the Eusebian system (see Hill, *First Chapters*, 55). Coogan (*Eusebius the Evangelist*, 165) observes that Epiphanius's reference to the 1,162 chapters also assumes his Greek-speaking audience is familiar with the apparatus.

5. Four-Gospel Codices

By Jerome's day, of course, the Gospels were normally encountered as joined together in codices, and they had been for a long time. At least by the 260s, the church in Caesarea, Palestine, was using a single volume containing all the Gospels (Eusebius, *Hist. eccl.* 7.15.4). That Jerome is even conscious of the codicological dimension when he thinks of the fourfold Gospel is indicated in some of his statements cited above. Among his descriptions of the four Gospels in his letter 53.9 to Paulinus is his assertion that the Gospels "hold together each by each and are interwoven one with another (*tenant se mutuo, sibique perplexi sunt*),"[86] words adapted from Ezek 1:9, "their wings touched each other";[87] or 1:11, "each of which touched the wing of another." What Ezek 1:9 and 11 said about the wings of the cherubim, that they touched or were "joined" (*junctaeque; iungebantur*) to each other, when applied to the four Gospels, would seem to refer to their being joined together, materially, in the formats in which late fourth-century readers would have been accustomed to seeing and using them.[88] This is

---

86. *PL* 22.548. Cf. the wings of the cherubim touching each other in the inner sanctuary of Solomon's temple (1 Kgs 6:27). In the same letter Jerome says that Ezra and Nehemiah are "united in a single book" (*in unum volume coarctantur*) (*PL* 22.548) and that the writings of the twelve prophets "are compressed within the narrow limits of a single volume" (*in unius voluminis angustias coarctati*) (PL 22.546).

87. The Hebrew is חֹבְרֹת אִשָּׁה אֶל־אֲחוֹתָהּ כַּנְפֵיהֶם. These words were not in the LXX— at least they are not in B. Alexandrinus has a form of them but takes the "touching" to refer to the faces: εχομεναι ετερα της και τα προσωπα αυτων; Origen added εχομεναι ετερα της και αι πτερυγες αυτων under the asterisk in his Hexapla (Rahlfs, *Septuaginta*). Jerome restored the words for Latin readers in his new translation: *iunctaeque errant pinnae eorum alterius ad alterum*.

88. It seems quite likely that Jerome's words "interwoven one with another" might be alluding to the Eusebian sections and canons that Jerome had supplied with his translation. Eusebius's invention was a key feature of Jerome's new edition. As Coogan says, Jerome even "adapted part of Eusebius' *Epistle to Carpianus* for his dedicatory epistle to Pope Damasus, the *Novum opus*. Jerome's letter to Pope Damasus was used extensively as a Gospel preface and was absorbed into later pedagogical projects of Gospel introduction. As a result, the Eusebian canons and the questions of comparative Gospel reading that they

confirmed in Jerome's *Commentary on Ezekiel*, written perhaps twenty years later,[89] where he says explicitly that

> The Gospels are *joined* to each other, and they are rooted in each other (*Juncta sibi sunt Evangelia haerentique mutuo*),[90] and in their flight they run here and there throughout the whole world. And they do not have an end to their flight, nor are they ever defeated and fall back, but they always advance to higher places.[91]

Jerome wrote well after our present, material evidence demonstrates that four-Gospel codices were in use; Irenaeus, however, wrote some time before it. But this could simply be because our extant evidence is so scant.[92]

After the discovery of P45 (holding all four Gospels and Acts), which he dated to the first half of the third century, Frederick Kenyon remarked, "it is now possible to believe that he [Irenaeus] may have been accustomed to the sight of volumes in which all four were contained."[93] Skeat thought that Irenaeus not only knew four-Gospel codices, but that "he used a source which had the four Gospels in the so-called 'Western' order of Matthew, John, Luke, Mark, which implies that all four were in a codex."[94] As noted above, I am not at all convinced that we can say Irenaeus used such a source, but his knowledge of four-Gospel codices is still, I think, extremely likely.

---

imply became central to Gospel reading in Latin" (Coogan, *Eusebius the Evangelist*, 126).

89. Between 410 and 414 (*NPNF*² 6:499).

90. He goes on to say, "they are all rooted in each other and are reckoned as a single corpus."

91. *PL* 25.24 (Scheck's translation [*St. Jerome*, 24–25]).

92. Even though the majority of papyrus Gospel fragments recovered are from single-Gospel codices, Skeat argued that these still presuppose a four-Gospel codex; otherwise, what would motivate a Christian reader to "abandon the practice of a lifetime and choose the codex" ("Origin," 83) over the roll as a means of carrying even a single Gospel? It is a simple but surprisingly compelling argument. Skeat neglected to consider the possibility, however, that a Pauline letter collection in codex form had already provided a model for a Gospel collection.

93. Kenyon, *Chester Beatty*, 13.

94. Skeat, "Origin," 80.

Now to a curious phrase of Irenaeus's, one that Skeat did not notice. In his description of the four living creatures in *Haer.* 3.11.8, Irenaeus says that Christ gave us "the Gospel as four-formed (τετράμορφον τὸ εὐαγγέλιον) but held together (συνεχόμενον) by the one Spirit."[95] Now, if one wanted to claim the common inspiration of the four Gospels, one might speak, as the Muratorian Fragment does, of everything in them being "declared by the one sovereign (*principali*) Spirit" (lines 16–17). But why would Irenaeus say that the four-formed Gospel (singular) itself is "held together"[96] by the one Spirit? It sounds uncannily like Jerome's comment two centuries later, that the four Gospels are "joined together."[97] Irenaeus certainly believed in a spiritual unity of the four, but why speak of the Gospel, in four books, as "held together" at all unless, like Jerome, he is thinking of these books as being held together in a codex?[98]

---

95. My translation (φανερωθεὶς τοῖς ἀνθρώποις ἔδοκεν ἡμῖν τετράμορφον τὸ εὐαγγέλιον, ἑνὶ δὲ Πνεύματι συνεχόμενον). The Latin translator has *declaratus hominibus, dedit nobis quadriforme Euangelium quod uno Spiritu continetur*. In the previous clause, Irenaeus has used the same word for "the Artificer of all things, the Logos, who sits upon the cherubim and holds all things together (ὁ . . . καὶ συνέχων τὰ πάντα)." Here, "holding all things together" fits well coming just after a reference to Christ the Word as the maker of all things (cf. *Haer.* 5.2.3; 5.18.3; Wis 1:7; Heb 1:2–3). But the four-formed Gospel being "held together" is different. Having just used the word, it springs again to Irenaeus's mind as he thinks of the physical form of the four Gospels.

96. The verb is used in a variety of ways in the LXX, but those instances that seem most relevant include Exod 26:3, where it is used for the curtains of the tabernacle being joined together (συνεχόμεναι); Exod 28:7; 36:11, 28, for the shoulder-pieces of the high priest's ephod being joined together (συνέχουσαι; συνεχούσας; συνεχομένους); and 1 Kgs 6:10, 15, where Solomon joined together (συνέσχεν) the partitions of the temple with cedar beams; and encompassed (συνεχόμενα) the inner parts of the temple with fir.

97. Irenaeus presumably would not have had Ezek 1:9 in his copy of the LXX, but he would have had 1:11.

98. Interestingly, the (probably only slightly later) Muratorian Fragment calls Luke "the third book of the Gospel (*tertium evangelii librum*)." This indicates a conception, much like that of Irenaeus, of the Gospel as one, in four books. And the phrase "third book of the Gospel" is quite compatible with—if it does not positively imply—the use of four-Gospel codices.

If Irenaeus did have a four-Gospel codex, it is not clear what sequence of the Gospels it had. Though he does (inadvertently) reveal the basis for the two main orders, he does not advocate for any order. And if he was working with a four-Gospel codex as he wrote *Against Heresies*, we should have to say it is most likely to have had Matthew first, then Luke, then Mark, and then John,[99] for he treats the Gospels' witness in this order on three occasions (*Haer.* 3.9.1–6; 3.11.7; 4.6.1). This would match the likeliest interpretation of Clement of Alexandria's tradition of the historical order of the Gospels' appearance (Eusebius, *Hist. eccl.* 6.14.5–7), and it is not necessarily incompatible with Irenaeus's historical listing in *Haer.* 3.1.1, where, although Mark is listed before Luke, the chronological priority is not definitively stated. In this passage Irenaeus began with the publication of Matthew's Gospel (in Hebrew) while Peter and Paul were preaching and laying the foundation of the church in Rome. Irenaeus then mentions Mark's Gospel before Luke's precisely because he had mentioned Peter before Paul in the previous sentence—Mark being the Gospel that hands down the preaching of Peter, and Luke the Gospel that preserves the preaching of Paul. I would judge that Irenaeus did not intend to state a definitive historical priority for Mark over Luke. But it does seem that later readers interpreted Irenaeus's words to mean just that.

6. *Concluding Summary*

Irenaeus found analogies for the fourfold Gospel in the four zones of the world, the four principal winds, and in the four living creatures of Ezekiel and Revelation. Viewed as logically necessary proofs for a "choice" of four and only four Gospels, his comparisons draw jeers. Understood as harmonizing ratifications

---

99. Commenting on the prevalence of this order in Irenaeus, Mutschler ("Irenäus und die Evangelien," 237) says "Am einfachsten liesse sich diese Reihenfolge dadurch erklären, dass sie seinem Bibelexemplar in einem Kodex zugrunde lag" ("The easiest way to explain this order is that it was based on his copy of the Bible in a codex"), as indeed was proposed long ago by J. Hoh, *Die Lehre*, 18. Mutschler accepts the real possibility of a four-Gospel codex by Irenaeus's time, based largely on Skeat's opinions.

from nature and Scripture for an entity already known and accepted, they had a much different effect upon early Christian readers. If it was Irenaeus who gave the cherubim-Gospel comparison its first articulation, we can say that he leveraged in a very successful way a familiar Christological reading of an evocative Old Testament conception of God in order to defend the apostolic Gospel from those who, in his mind, attempted to subtract from it or add to it. Because it is Jesus Christ, the Son of God and divine Word, who sits enthroned above the cherubim, the cherubim's four faces can be seen as depicting aspects of the manifestation of the Christ, which David petitioned:[100] his humble, incarnate humanity; his royal deity; his priestly work; and his possession and dispensing of the prophetic Spirit. "Now the Gospels harmonize with these, on which Christ Jesus is enthroned," says Irenaeus, and the harmony may be seen to consist not merely in a parallel, fourfold unity but in an analogous Christological import and sacred function. And even if the specific correlations made by Irenaeus are disputed, and even changed, his analogy retains great value. First, in the same way in which each one of Ezekiel's four cherubim had all four faces, each Gospel teaches all four aspects of the working of Christ. So, it may be discussed which "face" of which Gospel depicts one of these aspects more perfectly, without losing the overall analogy of the four Gospels as harmonizing with what the living creatures symbolize about the Christ's manifestation. Second, simply from a reception history perspective, Irenaeus's expositions—whether praised or condemned—did deliver some of the earliest recorded insights into the literary-theological character of each Gospel. And these have never lost their interest.

The point at which the evolving technology of the codex could accommodate two or more complete Gospel books in the same codex was the point at which the order of the Gospels became an issue. At that point, no prescribed sequence seems to have existed (Irenaeus may have possessed a codex with the order Matthew, Luke, Mark, and John). The two most prominent sequences in the

---

100. *Mens.* 35, "four spiritual creatures which were composed of four faces, which typify the coming of the Messiah."

textual tradition can be said to be rooted either in historical (a perceived chronological order) or theological (a desire to place apostles first) concerns. And yet, both can also be linked to Ezekiel's vision by means of the two earliest and most prolific correlations Christian interpreters drew between the four Gospels and the four living creatures. Irenaeus did not advocate any order, but if copyists followed his correlations, they produced what we now know as the Western order. If they followed those later popularized by Epiphanius and more especially by Jerome, they produced the order that ultimately prevailed. Early Christian reflection on Ezek 1 (and related texts), predated all three writers, and probably predated the four-Gospel codex. This makes it hard to rule out the possibility that these correlations may have played a role in the rise of both the Western and the present canonical orders.

Jerome's words about the four Gospels being "joined" to each other has prompted a second look at Irenaeus's language about the fourfold Gospel being "held together" by the one Spirit. His use of this language most likely assumes the existence of four-Gospel codices, which would only add the missing physical dimension to his strong conception of the unity of the fourfold Gospel and his practice of sometimes citing simply "the Gospel" when citing any one of the four.[101]

Much of this, we can say, seems to have grown out of the early proclamation of Christ, the Word, as the one who sits enthroned upon the cherubim, whom David praised and Ezekiel beheld. For, as the Gospel itself teaches, no one has seen the Father at any time; it is the only-begotten God who has made him known.

---

101. E.g., *Haer*. 1.7.4; 4.20.6, and references to the singular Gospel written by plural apostles (3.5.1; 4.34.1).

Bibliography

Alexander, P. "3 (Hebrew Apocalypse of) Enoch (Fifth-Sixth Century A.D.). A New Translation and Introduction." In *The Old Testament Pseudepigrapha: Apocalyptic Literature and Testaments*, edited by James H. Charlesworth, 1:223–53. Garden City, NY: Doubleday, 1983.

Andrew of Caesarea, Commentary on the Apocalypse. Translated by Eugenia Scarvelis Constantinou. Washington: The Catholic University of America Press, 2001.

Allen, Leslie C. *Ezekiel 1–19*. WBC 28. Dallas: Word, 1994.

Bardy, G., ed. *Eusèbe de Césarée: Histoire ecclésiastique*. 4 vols. Paris: Cerf, 1984–2001.

Briggman, Anthony. "Re-evaluating Angelomorphism in Irenaeus: The Case of 'Proof of the Apostolic Preaching' 10." *JTS* 61 (2010) 583–95.

Bruce, F. F. "The Earliest Latin Commentary on the Apocalypse." *EQ* 10 (1936) 352–66.

Constantinou, Eugenia S. *Guiding to a Blessed End: Andrew of Caesarea and his Apocalypse Commentary in the Ancient Church*. Washington, DC: The Catholic University of America Press, 2013.

Coogan, Jeremiah. *Eusebius the Evangelist. Rewriting the Fourfold Gospel in Late Antiquity*. Oxford: Oxford University Press, 2023.

Dean, James Elmer, ed. *Epiphanius' Treatise on Weights and Measures. The Syriac Version*. Studies in Ancient Oriental Civilization 11. Chicago: The University of Chicago Press, 1935.

Eskola, Timo. *Messiah and the Throne: Jewish Merkabah Mysticism and Early Christian Exaltation Discourse.* Tübingen: Mohr Siebeck, 2001. Reprint, Dallas: Fontes, 2019.

Ford, J. Massyngberde. *Revelation. A New Translation with Introduction and Commentary*, Anchor Bible Commentary. New York: Doubleday, 1975.

Funk, Robert W. "The Once and Future New Testament." In *The Canon Debate*, edited by Lee Martin McDonald and James A. Sanders, 541–57. Peabody, MA: Hendrickson, 2000.

Gamble, Harry. *The New Testament Canon: Its Making and Meaning.* Philadelphia: Fortress, 1985.

Hall, Stuart George, ed. *Melito of Sardis: On Pascha and Fragments.* Oxford Early Christian Texts. Oxford: Clarendon, 1979.

Hengel, Martin. "The Four Gospels and the One Gospel of Jesus Christ." In *The Earliest Gospels. The Origins and Transmission of the Earliest Christian Gospels—The Contribution of the Chester Beatty Gospel Codex P45*, edited by Charles Horton, 361–69. London: T. & T. Clark, 2004.

Hill, Charles E. "The *Epistula Apostolorum*: An Asian Tract from the Time of Polycarp." *Journal of Earley Christian Studies* 1 (1999) 1–53.

———, *The First Chapters: Dividing the Text of Scripture in Codex Vaticanus and Its Predecessors.* Oxford: Oxford University Press, 2022.

———. "The Gospel of John." In *The Oxford Handbook of Early Christian Biblical Interpretation*, edited by Paul M. Blowers and Peter W. Martens, 602–25. Oxford: Oxford University Press, 2019.

———. *The Johannine Corpus in the Early Church*. Oxford: Oxford University Press, 2004.

Hoh, J. *Die Lehre des hl. Irenäus über das Neue Testament*. Münster: Verlag der Aschendorffschen Verlagsbuchhandlung, 1919.

Houghton, H. A. G. *The Latin New Testament: A Guide to its Early History, Texts, and Manuscripts*. Oxford: Oxford University Press, 2016.

Irenaeus of Lyons. *Against the Heresies Book 3*. Ancient Christian Writers 64. Translated and annotated by Dominic J. Unger, with an Introduction and further revisions by Irenaeus M. C. Steenberg. New York/Mahwah, NJ: Newman, 2012.

———. *Against the Heresies Books 4 & 5*. Ancient Christian Writers 72. Translated and annotated by Dominic J. Unger, with an Introduction and further revisions by Scott D. Moringiello. New York/Mahwah, NJ: Newman, 2024.

Jerome. *Commentary on Ezekiel*. ACW 71. Translated by Thomas P. Scheck. New York/Mahwah, NJ: Newman, 2017.

———. *Commentary on Matthew*. Translated by Thomas P. Scheck. Washington: The Catholic University of America Press, 2008.

Kelly, J. N. D. *Jerome: His Life, Writings, and Controversies*. Peabody, MA: Hendrickson, 1988.

Kenyon, Frederick G. *The Chester Beatty Biblical Papyri: Descriptions and Texts of Twelve Manuscripts on Papyrus of the Greek Bible*, 3 fascicles, fascicle I, *General Introduction*. London: Oxford University Press, 1933.

The Lexham English Septuagint. Bellingham, WA: Lexham, 2019.

Lienhard, Joseph T. "Canons and Rules of Faith." In *The Oxford Handbook of Early Christian Biblical Interpretation*, edited by Paul M. Blowers and Peter W. Martens, 55–70. Oxford: Oxford University Press, 2019.

Metzger, Bruce. *The Canon of the New Testament: Its Origin, Development, and Significance*. Oxford: Clarendon, 1987.

McDonald, Lee Martin. *The Biblical Canon: Its Origin, Transmission, and Authority*. Peabody, MA: Hendrickson, 2007.

Mutschler, Bernhard. "Irenäus und die Evangelien." In *Gospels and Gospel Traditions in the Second Century: Experiments in Reception*, edited by Jens Schröter et al., 217–52. BZntW 235. Berlin: de Gruyter, 2020.

Patterson, Stephen J. *The Gospel of Thomas and Christian Origins: Essays on the Fifth Gospel*. Nag Hammadi and Manichaean Studies 84. Leiden: Brill, 2013.

Patton, Andrew J. "Greek Catenae and the 'Western' Order of the Gospels." *NovT* 64 (2022) 115–29.

Pearse, Roger, ed. *Origen of Alexandria: Exegetical Works on Ezekiel. The Fourteen Homilies and the Greek Fragments of the Homilies, Commentaries and Scholia*. Translated by Mischa Hooker. Ipswich: Chieftain, 2014.

Rahlfs, Alfred, ed. *Septuaginta. Id est Vetus Testamentum graece iuxta LXX interpretes*. Stuttgart: Deutsche Bibelgesellschaft, 1935, 1979.

Richard, M. "Témoins grecs des fragments XIII et XV de Méliton de Sardes." *Le Muséon* 85 (1972) 309–36.

Robinson, J. Armitage. "Selected Notes of Dr Hort on Irenaeus' Book III." *JTS* 33 (1932) 141–66.

Rothschild, Clare K. *The Muratorian Fragment: Text, Translation, Commentary*. Studien und Texte zu Antike und Christentum 132. Tübingen: Mohr Siebeck, 2022.

Rousseau, Adelin, ed. *Irénée de Lyon: La Démonstration de la Prédication Apostolique*. Sources Chrétiennes 406. Paris: Editions du Cerf, 1995.

Rousseau, Adelin, and L. Doutreleau, eds. *Contre Les Hérésies: Livre 3*. 2 vols. Sources Chrétiennes 210–11. Paris: Éditions du Cerf, 1974.

Saydon, P. P. "The Order of the Gospels." *Scripture* 4 (1950) 190–96.

Schmidt, Carl, and Isaak Wajnberg. *Gespräche Jesu mit seinen Jüngern nach den Auferstehung: Ein katholisch-apostolisches Sendschreiben des 2. Jahrhunderts*. Leipzig: J. C. Hinrichs, 1919.

Skeat, T. C. "A Codicological Analysis of the Chester Beatty Papyrus Codex of Gospels and Acts (P45)." *Hermathena* 155 (1993) 27–43.

———. "Irenaeus and the Four-Gospel Canon." *NovT* 34 (1992) 194–99.

———. "The Origin of the Christian Codex." *ZPE* 102 (1994) 263–68.

Skeat, T. C. and B. C. McGing. "Notes on Chester Beatty Biblical Papyrus I (Gospels and Acts)." *Hermathena* 150 (1991) 21–25.

Slusser, Michael, ed. *Justin Martyr: Dialogue with Trypho*. Translated by Thomas B. Falls. Revised and with a new introduction by Thomas P. Halton. Washington, DC: The Catholic University of America Press, 2003.

Swete, Henry Barclay. *The Apocalypse of St John. The Greek Text with Introduction Notes and Indices*. 3rd ed. London: Macmillan, 1911.

Watson, Francis. *An Apostolic Gospel: The 'Epistula Apostolorum' in Literary Context*. Society for New Testament Studies 179. Cambridge: Cambridge University Press, 2020.

———. *Gospel Writing: A Canonical Perspective*. Grand Rapids: Eerdmans, 2013.

Weinrich, William C., ed. *Latin Commentaries on Revelation*. Ancient Christian Texts. Downers Grove, IL: IVP Academic, 2005.

Wiles, Maurice F. *The Spiritual Gospel: The Interpretation of the Fourth Gospel in the Early Church*. Cambridge: Cambridge University Press, 1960.

Zahn, Theodor. *Geschichte des neutestamentlichen Kanons*. Erlangen/Leipzig: Deichert, 1890.

PATROLOGY BEYOND SUSPICION:
HERMENEUTICS, HOLINESS, AND HOPE

Kevin M. Clarke
Sacred Heart Major Seminary, Detroit, MI, USA

1. *Introduction*[1]

Suspicion of received accounts is characteristic of the historico-critical method. It is part of that reassessment of primary sources and that reconstruction of the "facts" which has, in the twentieth century, rehabilitated thinkers once dismissed as heretics, and exposed feet of clay beneath the gilded images of saints and heroes of the faith. Our understanding of the past has been transformed; no longer can we give an account of the Church of the Fathers as if there were from the beginning a pristine orthodoxy from which heretics diverged. Though it has sometimes sat a little uneasily with faith commitments, we owe much to modern suspicion.[2]

Frances Young's words should strike a familiar chord to many readers of this journal with a background in biblical studies, but it may not be so well known to those entering patristics that the study of the Church Fathers has undergone the same programmatic skepticism to which the biblical text has been subjected. It should come as no surprise, however, that patristics is in the same boat as biblical theology. As with biblical theology, "suspicion" has become a widely used methodological tool for studying the

---

1. I would like to express my gratitude to Taylor O'Neill, Joshua Madden, and an anonymous reviewer for their editorial assistance with this essay. I also am grateful to Origen scholar John Solheid, for a number of our conversations about this topic. Finally, I am grateful to my colleague Dan Keating for presenting this paper at the Academy of Catholic Theology annual meeting in Washington in May 2024 in my absence due to family emergency.
2. Young, "From Suspicion and Sociology to Spirituality," 421.

history of early Christianity.³ At the time of her writing, Young points out that "most patristic scholarship has not yet noticed that it resides in an intellectual backwater," which is to say, in Young's view, under the influence of modernity's "arrogance" rather than postmodernity's potency to deconstruct and reassign meaning.⁴

Young's essay is a helpful tour through modern hermeneutics. She describes her own background as "a *pot-pourri* of Gadamer, Saussure, Foucault, Derrida, Ricoeur, Stanley Fish and others."⁵ While it would be helpful to explore each of those thinkers in connection with this topic, it is sufficient to consider Young's principle of suspicion in its own right, especially whether it is truly an adequate means of approaching the Fathers. Suspicion yields a hearty crop, but it does not always produce an edible one. This is not to pass judgment on solid historical research, as there certainly is a great deal of good work being published about the Fathers, but is suspicion truly a sound philosophical mode of interpretation?

Full disclosure: I am quite fond of the Church Fathers. Once when I was a youth, I was arguing with my parents about my doubts concerning some aspect of doctrine—what it was, I do not remember. My own father said that the Fathers were sure guides concerning matters of the faith, and they had taught such and such.

---

3. See also Clark's work, *History, Theory, Text*. There, Clark articulates some key starting points for historians of late antiquity. Therein, she writes, "As a species of intellectual historian, scholars of late ancient Christianity occupy an *advantageous position* when considerations of theory are at issue. Given the rhetorical and ideological nature of their materials, these scholars may *safely assume* that their texts lie in a *largely unknown* and *dubious* relation to the 'reality' of the ancient Church, and should often be approached with a *hermeneutic of suspicion* and by *reading against the grain* . . . what might their studies look like? Among the 'mental tools' that theory offers scholars of patristic Christianity in approaching these tasks are (1) an examination of "authorial function" that calls into question attributions of intention and context; (2) symptomatic and Derridean readings that attend to the gaps, absences, and aporias in texts; (3) ideology critique, especially helpful in unpacking the early Christian writers' representations of various 'Others,' including women; and (4) postcolonial discourse theory that helps to illuminate the ways in which Christianity and Empire intertwined" (169–70) (emphasis mine).

4. Young, "From Suspicion and Sociology to Spirituality," 423.
5. Young, "From Suspicion and Sociology to Spirituality," 425.

Years later, I first became drawn to the Fathers when I decided to do some spiritual reading soon after I had graduated from Roanoke College. I had a copy of St. Augustine's *Confessions* from my undergraduate studies. Being a youth who struggled with similar problems as did the young Augustine, I most certainly did not read it when it was assigned to me, but I did when the Spirit pressed me into the text. I was instantly struck by how timelessly true the words of Augustine were. I would come to understand that I wished to continue studying theology because I wanted to enter into this tradition of handing on the faith from one generation to another. From this moment, my theological predilections were given to the Fathers. As I continued to explore the writings of the Fathers, I did not read them as though they were untrustworthy, yet I would not say that I read the Fathers uncritically. Reservations about this or that matter would arise from my readings, at which point the broader Tradition would prove helpful. In this regard, Thomas Aquinas proved to be a masterful exemplar as to the correct mode of reading the Fathers, reading discerningly but with a generous spirit.

As my research took me into greater depth in patristics, I observed that patristics was suffering from many of the same difficulties as biblical theology. "Are we reading the same text?" biblical theologians often ask. Early Christianity and patristics scholars often ask one another the same question, especially when reading texts with those who do not share first principles. The scope of "early Christian studies" is broadening so widely that patristic theologians could very easily lose their focus, which should remain firmly fixed upon the Fathers themselves as well as their mind-set, which was Christ Jesus. A theologian of the Fathers knows that the Holy Spirit is alive in the church, animating her during difficult moments and guiding these illustrious and God-bearing men to the correct interpretation of the received truth. They were the servants of the truth because they were focused on divine things, or on, in the words of Dionysius the Areopagite, "suffering divine things" ($\pi\alpha\theta\grave{\omega}\nu\ \tau\grave{\alpha}\ \theta\epsilon\hat{\imath}\alpha$).[6] Their theology was a truly speculative one, as it was not concerned merely with the practical but consist-

---

6. Dionysius the Areopagite, *Divine Names* 2.9 (*PG* 3:648B).

ed in looking into the realities of the faith.[7] Their theological expositions were truly sapiential in that they were ordered to the life of holiness in love and truth. Commenting upon the shortcomings of the historical-critical method in his famous 1988 Erasmus Lecture, then-Cardinal Joseph Ratzinger said, "what is needed is a criticism of criticism, developed, not from outside, but simply from within, from critical thought's potential for self-criticism."[8] Patristics, similarly, must secure itself as a theological science with its own principles but also as a science that is in conversation with the human sciences.

In light of the convergences of so many different philosophies of history in "early Christian studies" today, this essay first delin-

---

7. While the manner of studying theology in our time has often asserted the subordination of the speculative to the practical, in truth it is the other way around. Speculative theology seeks as much as possible an elevated apprehension of the divinity as well as the unity of truths known to human reason and those revealed by God, particularly the mystery of the most Holy Trinity, the central mystery of divine revelation and our Catholic faith. Aquinas upholds this distinction early in the *prima pars* of the *Summa Theologiae (STh)*: *Sed contra, omnis scientia practica est de rebus operabilibus ab homine; ut moralis de actibus hominum, et aedificativa de aedificiis. Sacra autem doctrina est principaliter de Deo, cuius magis homines sunt opera. Non ergo est scientia practica, sed magis speculativa* ("Every practical science has to do with the human working of things, such as the moral science has to do with the acts of human beings and architecture with buildings. But sacred doctrine has foremostly to do with God, whose work is especially man. Therefore, sacred doctrine is not a practical science, but it is a speculative one especially") (*STh*, I, q. 1, a. 4, s.c.) (translation mine). Aquinas continues on, however, asserting the fundamental connectivity between the speculative and the practical: *sacra tamen doctrina comprehendit sub se utramque; sicut et Deus eadem scientia se cognoscit, et ea quae facit. Magis tamen est speculativa quam practica, quia principalius agit de rebus divinis quam de actibus humanis; de quibus agit secundum quod per eos ordinatur homo ad perfectam Dei cognitionem, in qua aeterna beatitudo consistit* ("nevertheless sacred doctrine encompasses both [the speculative and the practical], as God by the same knowledge knows himself and what he has made. Nevertheless, it is more speculative than practical, because it principally has to do with divine things rather than with human acts, even though by them a man is directed to the perfect knowledge of God, in which eternal happiness consists") (*STh*, I, q. 1, a. 4, resp.) (translation mine). For more on the relation of the practical to the speculative, see O'Neill, "Primacy of the Speculative."

8. Benedict XVI, "Biblical Interpretation in Conflict," 100.

eates the scope of patrology, or the study of the Fathers, which aims at establishing the authority and authenticity of the works of the Fathers. Next, the essay explores some of the consequences for the study of "early Christianities" operating in a boundless pluralism and fatherlessness towards which it has been moving. Since the notion of "early Christianities" is stretched to its limits in the case of early gnosticism, the following section will consider Irenaeus's opponents. Irenaeus himself provides a particularly clever example that illustrates the importance of understanding the faith as something received as revealed by God, and his antiquity is especially useful for our purposes. Finally, the essay will propose a number of ways forward for patrology.

Above all, I would like to propose a way forward for patrology much like what Cardinal Ratzinger proposed for biblical studies in his famous Erasmus lecture: a criticism of criticism. I wish to do this in small part in this essay by my critique of suspicion. The study of the Fathers has much to gain from the fields of history, archaeology, sociology, philology, and so on, but the study of the Fathers is above all an ecclesial discipline.[9] The Fathers are indispensable sources for the Tradition—especially in the areas of doctrinal development and the interpretation of Scripture. As an ecclesiological discipline, it requires the freedom and the space to operate within its own theological principles unrestrained by the gate-keeping tendencies of academics who may not have the same regard for those to whom theologians owe the benefit of the doubt.

2. Delineating Patrology

First, let us have a look at how patrology has been classically understood. *Patrology* has been a field of theological inquiry for

---

9. See, for example, its centrality in the formation of future priests as articulated by the United States Conference of Catholic Bishops ("Patristic studies constitute an essential part of theological studies. Theology should draw from the works of the Fathers of the Church because of their lasting value within the living Tradition of the Church. The core should include patrology [an overview of the life and writings of the Fathers of the Church] and patristics [an overview of the theological thought of the Fathers of the Church]") (see *Program of Priestly Formation*, n327).

a couple of centuries, as evidenced by the existence of numerous patrological manuals. Patrology is the study of the Fathers (οἱ πατέρες). The Fathers were those men whose writings attained an authoritative status on matters of the development of doctrine in the conciliar era of the early church and beyond.[10] As William A. Jurgens stated, patrology concerns itself with "the study of the lives, doctrines, and writings of the Fathers of the Church."[11] This division is very well stated, since it is not only the study of the Fathers themselves with which patristics is concerned but also the study of their writings and teachings. How did one come to be recognized as a Father? Jurgens gives four criteria by which one can be considered a Father: "a) orthodox doctrine, b) sanctity of life, c) antiquity, and d) approval of the Church."[12] While the criteria seem simple enough, in practice, each of the Fathers finds himself on something of a spectrum with respect to each.

Patrology, like any field of study, struggles to set boundaries around its subjects. Too broad a field of study dilutes the results of inquiry. When, however, these four criteria above are applied strictly, the field of Church Fathers becomes narrow. But this is not without its own difficulties, as disputes quickly arise. Who are the Fathers of the Church? That is a difficult question to answer. Lists will vary depending on one's confession. Especially as early Christian studies open new vistas in ancient writings—such as those in Syriac, Armenian, Arabic, and so on—the question becomes even more difficult to answer. Certainly, orthodoxy stands

---

10. The question of early Christian women's influence upon the development of doctrine and upon the Fathers themselves is an important one, though beyond the scope of this essay. Select studies include Cohick and Hughes, *Christian Women*; Miller, ed., *Women in Early Christianity*; and Brock and Harvey, *Holy Women*.

11. Jurgens, *Faith of the Early Fathers*, x.

12. Jurgens, *Faith of the Early Fathers*, x. Hubertus Drobner points out that the category of antiquity is generally accepted by patristics scholars but that there is a degree of variation as to what constitutes "antiquity" with respect to the patristic era. Drobner suggests that the patristic era ends in the mid- to late fifth century, but this position is untenable as it would exclude John of Damascus, Germanus of Constantinople, Andrew of Crete, Maximus the Confessor—perhaps even Gregory the Great—and many others (Drobner, *Fathers of the Church*, 3–6).

out as a key criterion for determining whether an ancient figure could be considered a Church Father. But the criteria become difficult to manage in specific cases.

For example, no one would doubt the significance of Origen, but disputes could arise as to whether he could be considered a Church Father. Those arguing against his status as "Father" would say that he advanced doctrines that were not orthodox, that his life may not have been as saintly as imagined, and that he was rejected in the anathemas of the Second Council of Constantinople. Others eager to make room for Origen's status would argue that his theological difficulties were within fair theoretical boundaries, that he was a man of the church, and that his doctrine and exegesis was so influential among the approved Fathers that he could be considered as approved by the church. "The anathemas against him were illegitimately promulgated at Constantinople II," his supporters will argue. "Even if that were the case, the subsequent legitimate anathemas at later councils were not," his opponents will respond. Similar conversations occur with respect to others considered Fathers.[13] There is a certain awkward necessity, however, in pursuing those ends. J. Tixeront suggested distinguishing between the "Fathers" and those who are "ecclesiastical writers," but he argued correctly that there is a tolerable practical application of the word "Father" to those thinkers who were in error on this or that point.[14] Bernard Schmid makes a trifold distinction between Fathers, who meet the four criteria; ecclesiastical writers, who "though living in the communion of the Church have yet not always in their lives and writings expressed her pure and genuine traditional doctrine"; and Christian writers, "who have left behind writings on matters of the faith but who did not live in the communion of the Church."[15]

---

13. This is certainly not the place to adjudicate the cases of Clement of Alexandria, Evagrius of Ponticus, Didymus the Blind, and Diodore of Tarsus, much less those of Tertullian, Theodore of Mopsuestia, Jacob of Serug, Severus of Antioch, and others.

14. Tixeront, *Handbook*, 2.

15. Schmid, *Manual of Patrology*, 26–27. Among the "ecclesiastical writers," Schmid lists Clement of Alexandria, Origen, Tertullian, Lactantius, Eusebius, Rufinus of Aquileia, John Cassian, and Theodoret of Cyrus. He

Now, in attempting to delimit the study of patrology, Tixeront places it within the field of history, but what he meant by history in the early twentieth century could perhaps better be described by the phrase "historical theology," itself a difficult term, as evident below. He says, *"Patrology* is the study of the life and works of the men designated by that name [Father]. As a science, then, it is part of the history of Ancient Christian Literature, since it excludes from the field of its labors both the canonical writings of the New Testament and all writings that are strictly and entirely heretical."[16] He does recognize practical value in studying the heterodox works, which offer something of a clarification by contrast and help to shed light on the theological concerns of the Fathers.

While Tixeront has a more historical focus, Schmid takes a theological turn in his definition of patrology. He writes, "By Patrology is meant a systematic treatment and exposition of such preliminary subjects and questions as are necessary to acquire a proper knowledge of the writings of the Fathers, *and to make proper use of them in theology.*"[17] While one could study Thomas Aquinas out of mere historical curiosity, a better motivation for studying Thomas would be so that one can learn about the mysteries of the faith. Why should this not also be the case with the Fathers? Schmid distinguished patrology from the science of patristics, in that its object was the systematic arrangement of what could be harvested from the works of the Fathers, and from the history of ancient Christian literature, "because the latter includes the literary works not only of the Fathers, but also of the other ancient ecclesiastical writers."[18]

---

acknowledges that Irenaeus (chiliasm) or Gregory of Nyssa ("Origenist ideas") are to be counted among the Fathers "because they did not propound their opinions apodictically as the teaching of the Church." Schmid gives Novatian as an example of a "Christian writer."

16. Tixeront, *Handbook*, 2.
17. Schmid, *Manual of Patrology*, 19 (emphasis mine).
18. Schmid, *Manual of Patrology*, 19.

Having defined patrology, Schmid delineates its threefold object:

> The object, therefore, of Patrology, in this narrow sense, is, in the first place, to lay down and establish the rules and principles which help to determine the authority of the Fathers and the authenticity, right use, and application of their works in theology. In the next place, its object is to give some account of the life education, mental training, literary and pastoral work of each of the Fathers, also to determine their precise position in the Church, with their relative merits in ecclesiastical science. A further duty of Patrology is to explain the substance, scope, and number of their writings, the peculiarity of their view, their style of writing, and, finally, to indicate the best editions of their works.[19]

In sum, authentic patrology strives to establish the authority of the Fathers and the authenticity of their works, briefly narrates their story, and sets them apart according to their uniqueness and gifts—all with a theological end in view.

3. *Early Christianities and New First Principles*

But perhaps one of the key difficulties for patrology is that not enough emphasis has been laid upon discovering theological wisdom in the Fathers. The speculative and sapiential elements of theology have been neglected in favor of a host of other pursuits. Indeed, the field has grown suspicious of terms such as "orthodoxy" and "heresy"—or, according to Elizabeth Clark, "what was for-

---

19. Schmid, *Manual of Patrology*, 19–20. By way of comparison, consider Joseph T. Lienhard's helpful description of the object of historical theology, albeit a discipline that has a scope encompassing all of Christian history. He writes, "The object of historical theology includes not only the public expressions of Christian faith (for example, baptismal creeds and the liturgy) and of the Church's doctrine (for example, conciliar creeds and the dogmatic decrees of the councils), but also the writings of theologians—that is, the thought and ideas of learned Christians (taken in a sense broad enough to include writings on exegesis, morality, spirituality, and similar areas) on how to understand and synthesize the Church's teaching and relate it to other questions and concerns" ("Historical Theology," 271).

merly labelled 'heresy.'"[20] Patrology has always benefitted from interdisciplinary conversations with other sciences, but perhaps patrology's greatest fault in recent decades is that it has at times failed to keep those outside influences from redefining patrology's very object of study, as detailed above. While patrology as a theological discipline should be fairly clear in its delimitation, a new tide of scholarship is changing the face of the study of the Fathers in our day. It boasts of a philosophy of history that has made inroads into the study of the Fathers, a philosophy suggesting that skepticism about established narratives enables one to deconstruct and rewrite those narratives. Scholars favor the phrase "early Christianity" in place of patristics. Even the phrase "early church" has come under the suspicion of historians. Instead, "Christianity in late antiquity" has become preferred.[21] After all, "early church" presupposes a unified whole, and it was anything but unified or whole, they argue.

The terminological differences may seem inconsequential, but within this movement is a strong self-assertion from historians within the field. Averil Cameron, who describes herself as "a historian, not a patristics theologian" in her article "The Cost of Orthodoxy," wrote that "it is more important now than ever to be

---

20. Clark, "From Patristics to Early Christian Studies," 22. See also Henry, "Why Is Contemporary Scholarship so Enamored of Ancient Heretics?" Clark summarizes this work, writing "social challenges to 'authority' in the 1960s encouraged the view within early Christian studies that 'orthodoxy' was oppressive and its challengers ('heretics') more interesting and worthy of study" ("From Patristics to Early Christian Studies," 22); cf. Cameron, "Cost of Orthodoxy."

21. Bart Ehrman and Andrew Jacobs characterize the term "Early Church" along evolutionary lines, suggesting that the term means "a single organism that evolved from the simple ministry of Jesus and the apostles into the institutionally and theologically complex system of clergy, canons, and creeds that became the dominant religion of the Mediterranean world." In the history of ideas, such a simple-to-complex characterization is in greater debt to Martin Luther and Immanuel Kant than it is to Charles Darwin. Nevertheless, the evolving organism account enables Ehrman and Jacobs to codify their terminological shift: "If the study of the Early Church was the study of religious evolution—organic, holistic, and self-contained—then the study of Christianity in Late Antiquity has become the study of religious revolution: unpredictable, multifaceted, and diverse" (see Ehrman and Jacobs, eds., *Christianity in Late Antiquity*, 1).

aware of the relations, and the tensions, between confessional and non-confessional scholarship."[22] Historical scholarship is non-confessional, in Cameron's view, and so the field becomes more navigable if some key distinctions, such as the difference between orthodoxy and heresy, are dissolved. Cameron has identified two different views of orthodoxy, which she calls the essentialist and the constructivist, the former viewing orthodoxy as a given and necessarily adjusts and reacts to the rise of heresies, the latter viewing orthodoxy as "emerging from a mass of competing versions."[23] This latter constructivist approach is most characterized by Walter Bauer, who alleges that heresy generally precedes orthodoxy. Bauer rejects what he calls the "ecclesiastical position," which is bound up with the notion of the *regula fidei*, the rule of faith that the church has preserved intact from the teachings of Christ himself. Bauer sees expression of the ecclesiastical position in the words of Origen, "All heretics at first are believers; then later they swerve from the rule of faith." Bauer finds such an assertion unhistorical. He argues that historical criticism "all too easily submits to the ecclesiastical opinion as to what is early and late, original and dependent, essential and unimportant for the earliest history of Christianity."[24] A logical consequence is that heresy

22. Cameron, "Cost of Orthodoxy," 339–40.
23. Cameron, "Cost of Orthodoxy," 344–45.
24. Bauer, *Orthodoxy and Heresy*, xxiii–xxiv. Bauer cites First Clement as evidence that ecclesiastical authorities in Rome imposed orthodoxy on other communities of the Mediterranean (229). Citing Bock against this, Köstenberger and Kruger point out that Bauer's reading of First Clement greatly weakens his overall thesis about confessional pluralism among Christians because Bauer did not show that orthodoxy was only to be found in Rome and because he did not show that Clement was imposing rather than trying to convince. Köstenberger and Kruger bring forth six key reasons against this interpretation of Roman primacy (i.e., that orthodoxy is only to be found in Rome): (a) the origination of the monepiscopacy outside of Rome; (b) evidence of theological schisms in Antioch from Ignatius; (c) New Testament writings originating from Asia Minor that attest to orthodoxy already present there; (d) Marcion's activity in Sinope presupposes an antecedent orthodoxy in the works he drew from; (e) the earliest sources on the liturgy are Syrian; and (f) Pliny the Younger reports of Christ-worshippers in Bithynia in a letter to Trajan (see Köstenberger and Kruger, *Heresy of Orthodoxy*, 50–52); cf. Bock, *Missing Gospels*, 50–51.

and heretics are imposed sociological constructs for self-differentiation. If there is no received *regula fidei*, there can be no departure from it.

In her work on the second-century heretic Marcion, Judith Lieu denies that Marcion was actually a heretic, but that he was only "made" into a "heretic," an idea that "is a construction of early Christian rhetoric within the processes of shaping some form of self-definition or identity."[25] In contrast to the Fathers' perspective, Lieu considers Marcion "a thoroughly Christian thinker," saying that "for him, his 'myth' or account of the need, solution, and response of salvation were to be found within the distinctively Christian authorities."[26] While confessional Christians would cringe at the notion of considering Marcion a Christian, this is well-within the bounds of an ever-expanding sense of Christian pluralism that results from Bauer's project. If, however, one were to ask one of the early Fathers whether Marcion was made into a heretic, he might say, "Yes. Marcion made himself a heretic, even a heresiarch."[27] At any rate, the expanding contemporary histori-

25. Lieu, *Marcion*, 433.
26. Lieu, *Marcion*, 436. Marcion's received authorities—compared with the early Christian writers—were quite narrow in scope, limited to much of Paul's writings and some of Luke. On some level, he appears to accept the Old Testament as revealed truth, but he refuses to accept harmony between Old and New. This, however, does not really make Marcion "a thoroughly Christian thinker" but only a *partially* Christian thinker, which is something that could be said for all heretics.
27. Despite his hatred for the law of Moses and his rejection of the Old Testament, Marcion manages to carry the allure of a rebel ahead of his time. As the project of recovering the historical figure of Marcion advances, many scholars will not find an enlightened renaissance man, rather, if the Fathers' characterization of him is correct, a staunchly rigid anti-Jewish thinker. He rejects the religion of the Old Testament outright, which elicited a very strong response from second-century apologists. To circumnavigate the historical problem of an established orthodoxy preceding Marcionism, some contemporary scholars are postponing New Testament writings. Markus Vinzent attempts to date not only the writings of the New Testament into the second century, but even the entire genre of Gospel alongside and in response to Marcion. Not only was Marcion extremely influential in the second century, Vinzent even goes so far as to say that "he marks the transition from an oral memory of Jesus's oracles and perhaps some 'retelling of inherited narratives' of Jesus of Nazareth, to the written combination

cal position regards orthodoxy as a sort of empowered social construction. In such a view, Christianity in the time of the Fathers, also known as "proto-orthodoxy," is the outcome of historical movements and shifting power dynamics rather than the authentic transmission of a faith with a definite content, albeit in the early stages of doctrinal development.

Along these lines, Clark observed,

> How did 'patristics' become 'early Christian studies' in the late twentieth century, and how did 'early Christian studies' itself develop to adopt new modes of analysis? Several factors—most prominently exhibited in North America—fostered the change in conception and nomenclature. The term 'patristics' fell increasingly into disuse, taken as a sign of ecclesiasticism, maleness, and 'orthodoxy', from which some scholars wished to dissociate themselves. Yet the more traditional topics—philology, theology, exegesis, historical studies—continued to flourish, sometimes taking surprising turns.[28]

---

of oracles and similes of the Lord, and in this sense, because the author of his Gospel, which was *the first Gospel of its kind*" (*Marcion*, 158) (emphasis mine). Vinzent intends this literally, that is, before the other four Gospels were composed. He admits that he "dared to venture the idea that he himself was the first Gospel writer" (157). Elsewhere, he writes, "Marcion, who *created* the new literary genre of the 'Gospel' and also gave his work this title, had *no historical precedent* in the combination of Christ's sayings and narratives" (277) (emphases mine). This latter quote presupposes a great deal, such as a very late genesis of all the narrative traditions.

28. Clark, "From Patristics to Early Christian Studies," 14. Later, Clark gives a couple of examples of theology that she considers "more satisfactorily" harmonious with the new directions in the field. She writes, "Despite newer social and cultural approaches to the study of late ancient Christianity, it is not the case that theology has been abandoned. In some quarters, theology and history are being more satisfactorily integrated to construct a genuinely *historical* theology. Here, an instructive example is offered by J. Rebecca Lyman's *Christology and Cosmology: Models of Divine Activity in Origen, Eusebius, and Athanasius* (1993). Later constructions of 'orthodoxy,' Lyman claims, provide no key to theological concerns of the second through mid-fourth centuries, and the imposition of such later models serves only to 'obscure the actual history of early Christianity' (Lyman 1993: 7, 161). Underscoring the diversity of early Christian theologies, Lyman invites readers to attend to how the varying cosmological models embraced by various early Christian writers correlate with the different communal settings in which they lived and worked, from urban study groups to an asceti-

In fact, as Clark and Cameron's essays suggest, we have witnessed a redefinition of the field altogether, or, as Charles Kannengiesser put it, "patristics breaking out of its former clerical and theological ghetto and extending its appeal to new categories of scholars."[29] This he said despite his great reverence for figures like Aloys Grillmeier, Henri de Lubac, Jean Daniélou, and others. We are well into this shift, quite visibly evident as more associations and journals shake the "patristics" label. In 2011, the South African journal *Acta Patristica et Byzantina* became the *Journal of Early Christian History*. Whether other organizations or publications go this route remains to be seen.[30] Despite Clark's optimism about room in the field for the traditional topics, the field of early Christian studies is less a conversation of dogmatic or speculative theology, but a sociocultural conversation about ecclesiastical and political power, the suppression of dissent, and so on. Classically understood, "orthodoxy" has become somewhat of an accident of history, or, to put it differently, "the history of Christianity has to be written regionally."[31] Implied in the movement toward the term "Christianities" is the fragmentation of the "one" faith. It is one thing to have a variety in the modes of expression of the one faith passed down from Christ through many apostles, but it is another thing altogether to regard the Valentinians, the Marcionites, the Arians, and others, as being a different but valid expression of the faith of Paul.

When I began interacting with scholars studying the Church Fathers from perspectives such as those listed above, I could not

---

cally oriented, and imperially established, ecclesia (Lyman 1993: 9, 162–4). The function of religious language in its social-historical setting is Lyman's overall concern. A second example of 'theology in a different mode' is Virginia Burrus's *'Begotten, Not Made': Conceiving Manhood in Late Antiquity* (2000). Far from abandoning the concept 'patristics,' Burrus pursues it with vigour, borrowing 'mental tools' from French feminist theory. Here, the fathers' 'masculine' Trinitarian language is interrogated with the tools of gender theory" ("From Patristics to Early Christian Studies," 23).

29. Kannengiesser, "Future of Patristics," 128.
30. The North American Patristics Society, for example, is well into a process of the re-evaluation of its own name.
31. King, "Which Early Christianity?" 69.

help but sense that we were talking past one another. That is not an indictment of non-theological approaches to the Church Fathers; that is not my purpose at all. I greatly value the many legitimate contributions to the study of the Church Fathers that historians, archeologists, anthropologists, philologists, and others provide. Interdisciplinary collaboration is quite necessary, to be sure. Theology itself, which as a *scientia* with its own principles and sources, gradually losing its pride of place when it comes to the study of the Church Fathers, must stand its ground. This task of recovering theology's space is most urgent. In the attempted marginalization of theology, with all its accompanying speculative rigors under the guiding stars of the contemplation of divine things and faith's confession, the mind of the Fathers becomes lost to the world. The result would be the disruption of the stream of Tradition that waters believers.

Some of the claims of social historians, as noted above, savor of triumphalism, as though early Christianities has won the day. Lest the reader think I am composing a dirge to patristics, I am not convinced. The experience on the ground at conferences, such as the North American Patristics Society, Oxford Patristics, the American Academy of Religion, and others, where very large groups of scholars from a variety of confessional backgrounds present patristic papers on theological topics, tells a different story. There has never been a better time to be a patrologist. New translations, resources, and initiatives (like this present journal) give theologians an overabundance of opportunities.

Patrology especially requires the scholar to make known his or her first principles from the outset. Many of us do not have the same reservations that social historians have about using terms like Fathers, early church, orthodoxy, heretic, and so forth. The terms all presuppose the reality of divine revelation, and that truth itself can be known. Terms such as these, as uncomfortable and unusable as they may be for some, help the theologian safeguard the *regula fidei*, which is part of the "ecclesial vocation of the theologian." While social historians have comfortably set them aside, it is not reasonable to expect that theologians would do likewise, especially in light of theology's speculative and practical dimensions as a *scientia*. It must be able to say what theology is and what it is not.

As theologians and social historians contest one another's interpretative claims over philosophical grounds, it is worth pausing over Cardinal Ratzinger's words to biblical exegetes, which could be directly applied to today's readers of the Church Fathers.

> The exegete must not approach the interpretation of the text with a ready-made philosophy or with the dictates of a so-called modern or "scientific" world view, which predetermines what may and may not be. He must not exclude, a priori, the possibility that God could speak, as himself, in human words in the world; he must not exclude the possibility that God, as himself, could act in and enter into history—however improbable this may seem to him. He must be ready to let himself be taught by the phenomenon itself. He must be ready to accept that this may occur in history: a real beginning, which cannot as such be derived from what was already given, but opens up from itself. Nor may he deny to man the capacity to hear things beyond the range of the categories of pure reason, the ability to transcend himself into the open and infinite truth of being.[32]

Similarly, if I were to adapt Ratzinger's quote modifying it for my own purposes, I would say that the reader of patristic texts should not predetermine the motives of the Church Fathers based on modern or postmodern assumptions. Such a reader should not *a priori* exclude the *theological* possibility that the Holy Spirit could guide the Tradition of the church through the ages or the possibility that these patristic witnesses could indeed be both virtuous and holy, "however improbable this may seem." Such a reader should be open to the notion that God has continued to work in history through particular agents who possessed a special charism to clarify the received Tradition given by Jesus Christ himself and passed down through the Apostles. An interpreter of the Fathers should not deny to others "the capacity to hear things

---

32. Benedict XVI, "Biblical Interpretation in Conflict," 116–17. Cameron criticizes Benedict for what she considers an "uncompromising stance" in the Regensburg lecture that Christianity cannot be removed from *logos*, or the "breadth of reason," arguing that Christianity is about much more than reason, such as "practice, social behaviour, emotion, *habitus*, worship, and more" (see Cameron, "Cost of Orthodoxy," 343–44) (emphasis original).

beyond the range of the categories of pure reason," power, identity differentiation, and the like, nor deny to others the notion that the Fathers had something in mind other than preserving for the good of souls the saving truth of the Incarnate Word, Jesus Christ, one of the Holy Trinity.

4. A Test Case: Are Irenaeus's Opponents Christians?

The difficulty with Bauer's constructivist notion of orthodoxy is this simple matter: orthodoxy becomes invention rather than gift. Or, to put it even more simply, orthodoxy is of human origin rather than divine. The question of truth becomes an investigation of one's own local customs rather than an inquiry into revelation. Irenaeus's *Adversus Haereses*, or more properly titled, *A Refutation and Overthrow of the Falsely Named Knowledge*, provides a unique example that helps prove the point I wish to make about theological wisdom and the pursuit of truth. From Irenaeus, we get the richest early Christian teachings of apostolic succession, though he was by no means the first to present such ideas. Clement of Rome, likely in the late first century articulates the theology concisely in his first letter to the Corinthians.[33] Irenaeus, like the scholastics who would come much later, has no hesitation to present the views of his opponents. It is obvious why he does this: Christians were departing from the community because of the enchanting magnetism of the gnostic preachers. The mystique of the teachers of gnosticism incited the curiosity of listeners and drew them from the Christian community in order to learn the much-coveted secret knowledge (γνῶσις). Irenaeus, therefore, devotes the first seven chapters of book 1 to the gnostic cosmology, and he does so with great detail and accuracy. He wishes to demonstrate that knowledge of their story sharply contrasts with the rule of faith.

Gnosticism has undergone a particular revival in our times.[34] Similarly, gnostic themes pervade popular documentaries and

---

33. See 1 Clem. 40–44 (Holmes, *Apostolic Fathers*).
34. See, O'Regan's work *Gnostic Return*, wherein O'Regan argues that gnostic thought pervades modern discourse. Of the revival of fascination with

movies about Christ.[35] Irenaeus would surely have lamented these phenomena, as he considers gnosticism not at all a form of Christianity. Irenaeus's exposition clearly shows how gnosticism is indeed closer to Greek polytheism. Interestingly, the pluralistic gnostics, who eagerly appropriate the Christian Scriptures to the project of their mythmaking, confront modern thinkers with a dilemma: were the gnostics Christians or not? They talk about Christ and fit him into their cosmology on their own terms, not His, all while denouncing the God of the Old Testament as inferior. Irenaeus shows us that the gnostics are not only outside the rule of faith (*regula fidei*), but that it is erroneous to consider them Christians because they in no wise follow Christ's teachings.

In the second century, Valentinus and his followers were leading astray many Christians by means of their deceptive interpretations of Scripture, Irenaeus tells us. To Irenaeus, it was not as though they were merely misinterpreting, but that this was a purposeful distortion of the revealed truth which had been passed down from the apostles. The real gem is an allegory found in chapter 8 of book 1. Now, when reading this, it is important to be mindful that the preceding seven chapters had been devoted to an exposition of the gnostic cosmogony, much of which they had drawn from the Christian Scriptures (Old and New Testaments). This particular allegory, by which Irenaeus masterfully captures the program of the heretics, is worth quoting at length:

> Such is their system which neither the prophets preached, nor the Lord taught, nor the apostles handed down. They boast rather loudly of knowing more about it than others do, citing it from non-scriptural works; and, as people would say, they attempt to braid ropes of sand. They try to adapt to their own sayings in a manner worthy of credence, either the Lord's parables, or the prophets' sayings, or the apostles' words, so that their fabrication might not appear to be with-out witness.

---

gnosticism in the popular culture, any visit to the "Christianity" section of Barnes & Noble will demonstrate this; there the label is applied quite liberally to gnostic and neo-gnostic texts.

35. See, for example, *The History Channel*'s 2003 Christmas documentary *Banned from the Bible*. In popular film, examples may be seen in Martin Scorsese's *Last Temptation of Christ* (1988) or more recently, Darren Aronofsky's *Noah* (2014).

> They disregard the order and the connection of the Scriptures and, as much as in them lies, they disjoint the members of the Truth. They transfer passages and rearrange them; and, making one thing out of another, they deceive many by the badly composed phantasy of the Lord's works words that they adapt. By way of illustration, suppose someone would take the beautiful image of a king, carefully made out of precious stones by a skillful artist, and would destroy the features of the man on it and change around and rearrange the jewels, and make the form of a dog, or of the fox, out of them, and that a rather bad piece of work. Suppose he would then say with determination that this is the beautiful image of the king that the skillful artist had made, at the same time pointing to the jewels which had been beautifully fitted together by the first artist into the image of the king, but which had been badly changed by the second into the form of a dog. And suppose he would through this fanciful arrangement of the jewels deceive the inexperienced who had no idea of what the king's picture looks like, and would persuade them that this base picture of a fox is that beautiful image of the king. In the same way these people patch together old women's fables, and then pluck words and sayings and parables from here and there and wish to adapt these words of God to their fables.[36]

Immediately these words confront a relativistic reading, which would suggest that the image of the king is of equal value to that of the dog or the fox. Perhaps that may be a modern tendency; after all, who is to say who is right these days? It is one thing to be sympathetic to the gnostics and wonder if accusations were embellished against them, but their cosmogony by any account liberally pulls quotes from the Scriptures out of context and apart from the author's intention. That is a very difficult thing for any scholar to defend, even if one has gnostic sympathies.

What are the consequences of this sort of reading? If the Scriptures are merely a human work, then the project of the gnostics to decode the Scriptures and reconstruct them for their own theological purpose is, at best, a distortion of the intention of the human authors of the Scriptures. To be sure, such a project is no light offense. By way of illustration, Irenaeus himself imagines this being done to the works of Homer, carefully arranging verses about various figures such as Priam, Menelaus, Agamemnon, and Odysseus

---

36. *Adversus Haereses* 1.8.1 (Unger, ACW).

in such a way so that they appear as if they were seamlessly describing the deeds of Hercules alone:

> When thus it had been spoken, there was sent from his house deeply groaning
> Hercules powerful hero, with brilliant deeds acquainted,
> By Eurystheus, the son of Sthenelus, Perseus's offspring,
> That from Erebus he might fetch the dog of dark Hades.
> So, like a mountain: bred lion he went, confident of his prowess,
> Rapidly through the city while all his friends followed after,
> Unmarried maidens and youths, also much experienced old men,
> Bitterly weeping for him as one going forward to death.
> Therefore Hermes together with blue-eyed Athena did send him;
> For she knew how the heart of her brother was suffering with grief.[37]

Each line is from a different place in the Homeric corpus but is arranged in such a way that the unlearned could think the newly created context refers to Hercules. Homer is thus rewritten, but contrary to Homer's own intention. Who would legitimize something like this in literary criticism? Even if one appreciates allegory, this is so far detached from the Homeric narrative as to become something completely estranged from his work. That is the effectiveness of the example for Irenaeus. Doing such to Homer is intellectually dishonest in itself. If, however, the Christian Scriptures are indeed divinely inspired, how much more is the offense since they are wisely arranged by the Artist! That is Irenaeus's point: the "skillful artist" is not the human author but the divine. That fact is plainly evident to anyone reading Irenaeus.

But how can one be sure that one reads the Scriptures in a way superior to the Valentinians? The heretics simply do not have the authority to engage in such a task. They begin already outside the boundary. That is the beauty of the "rule of truth," which for Irenaeus is a technical term of sorts to describe the unity of Scripture and Tradition. It was a sure anchor for the early church. Irenaeus explains:

> And each one of them claims as this wisdom that which he discovers by himself, which is really a fiction, so that their truth may fittingly be

---

37. *Adversus Haereses* 1.9.4 (Unger, ACW).

in Valentinus at one time, at another in Marcion, and another in Cerinthus, finally in Basilides, or even in one who disputes against these and would not be able to say anything pertaining to salvation. For each one of them, being totally corrupt, is not ashamed to deprave the rule of truth and preach himself.[38]

The truth is not accessible only to the few who had been enlightened. "All," Irenaeus says, "who wish to see the truth can view in the whole Church the tradition of the apostles that has been manifested in the whole world. Further, we are able to enumerate the bishops who were established in the Churches by the apostles, and their successors even to ourselves."[39] The Christian community itself is intrinsically linked to the apostolic office. Irenaeus and Clement of Rome before him stand in the patristic foreground in the development of the doctrine of apostolic succession. From Clement to Irenaeus, this doctrine swiftly matures with great necessity, especially in light of the heresies the early Christians encountered. Some modern scholars tend to view this matter merely sociologically. Such a way of thinking would suggest that apostolic succession was an idea that helped delimit the community very clearly as the church expanded and dealt with external and internal adversaries. This hermeneutic of history contributes indeed to our understanding of the development of the Christian community. Yet, the sociological historical perspective taken in isolation can be a retrojection, falling short of considering the authentic motives of the Fathers. Were first and second century Christians only trying to determine who was in their group and who was of the inauthentic faction? Was the description of the proper manner of the rites of Eucharist and Holy Orders a mere vehicle for defining the boundaries of the group? No, it was the other way around. At the heart of the matter is theology itself.

Irenaeus demonstrates that the church derives its sacred life from the succession from the apostles and from the bishops they appointed. The apostles "willed that the men whom they left behind as their successors and to whom they gave their own teaching

---

38. *Adversus Haereses* 3.2.1 (Unger, ACW).
39. *Adversus Haereses* 3.3.1 (Unger, ACW).

office should be perfect and blameless in every respect."[40] Irenaeus's opponents, on the other hand, freely boast that they know more than some of the apostles through their particular religious enlightenment. They claim to be superior to the apostles, and their own boast of separation is proof enough for Irenaeus to censure their "unauthorized assemblies." To consider the matter another way, "Before Valentinus, of course, the Valentinians did not exist; and before Marcion, there were no Marcionites."[41] For Irenaeus, the apostolic succession effects the deputing of the bishop for authentic preaching, and the lineage itself is a sort of sign that points to a deeper reality. Not only does Irenaeus make clear his understanding of Tradition's governance over biblical interpretation, but he also implies that each of the churches could trace their succession back to an apostle. Because the faith is something passed down, believers are part of an ancient church; thus, "every Church . . . should agree, because in her the apostolic tradition has always been safeguarded by those who are everywhere."[42]

Early Christian historian David Brakke attempts to challenge this conception, namely, that one could speak of a unified church in Irenaeus's time. It would not be unfair to detect here a note of "suspicion of received accounts," in Young's words. Brakke argues that between Irenaeus and Justin Martyr, for example, one finds just as much doctrinal diversity as between Valentinus and Basilides, and that to view an early Christianity that includes both Irenaeus and Justin as a unity is really only a privilege of post-Constantinian Christianity.[43] Brakke sees Justin as the inventor of the term "heresy," though he says Justin cannot make use of this "powerful tool" because he "lacked any authority to enforce his views" within the dynamics of community definition.[44] Irenaeus, however, being a bishop, does not lack the power to delimit boundaries between Christian and non-Christian. "In Irenaeus' programme, the bishop was responsible for *enforcing with practi-*

---

40. *Adversus Haereses* 3.3.1 (Unger, ACW).
41. *Adversus Haereses* 3.4.3 (Unger, ACW).
42. *Adversus Haereses* 3.2.1 (Unger, ACW).
43. Brakke, "Self-Differentiation," 246.
44. Brakke, "Self-Differentiation," 254.

cal measures the truth that he received from the apostles."[45] Brakke describes the function of the rule of faith as one of the early Christian "strategies of self-differentiation." The rule of faith itself serves "as a limit to such reading and speculation" that would go beyond normative readings of Scripture.[46] Brakke says that "Irenaeus and others hoped to eliminate diversity and establish a single church with a single truth."[47] Certainly, Brakke is correct that the *regula fidei* differentiated early Christians from their counterparts and that diversion from it necessitated a practical pastoral response.

Why, however, does Irenaeus exposit the gnostic cosmogony to the best of his knowledge and pit it against the notion of a received "rule of truth"? Rather than considering the gnostic exposition sociologically as a mere means of community self-differentiation, for Irenaeus, the exposition of gnostic mythologies, whether Valentinian or other, is fundamentally pastoral. As he writes in the preface to the work, Irenaeus gives insight into his purpose, "Thus, having learned of these mysteries yourself, you can make them clear to all your people and warn them to be on guard against this profundity of nonsense and of blasphemy against God."[48] He does not attempt to silence the gnostics, but brings their beliefs into full view as a means of pastoral defense against error. The truth is a defense. It is true that the rule of faith has a limiting function for biblical interpretation, but for Irenaeus it has an exact content that says more about what the faith is than what it is not. The notion that the rule of faith puts a limit upon speculation is difficult to square with the copious nature of Irenaeus's own speculative reflections in *Adversus haereses*, which traverse five lengthy books.

In the context of Irenaeus's day, there was a great risk that his flock would depart from the Christian community and join this

45. Brakke, "Self-Differentiation," 255 (emphasis mine).
46. Brakke, "Self-Differentiation," 259–60.
47. Brakke, "Self-Differentiation," 260. Irenaeus would certainly have challenged that assertion, presumably denying that he is trying to "establish a single church." In Irenaeus's view, he himself would not have such a consequential role—the church is already established by Christ. Further, Irenaeus recognizes a multiplicity of churches, but a unity of belief in the "rule of truth."
48. *Adversus Haereses* Preface (Unger, ACW).

spreading heresy. St. Jerome famously said that "ignorance of Scripture is ignorance of Christ."[49] Granted that many in the early church did not have the Scriptures readily accessible, they nonetheless illustrate the principle. Ignorance of Scripture meant they were susceptible to false teachers, like Valentinus, Marcion, and Basilides. Having knowledge of the Scriptures as handed down through the rule of faith (i.e., the Sacred Tradition that comes to us through the apostles) is the true knowledge (γνῶσις) that conducts one into the kingdom of God. The type of exegesis that the Fathers did was something like an observer in front of that great mosaic. He plainly sees the image of the king. As he looks at the image, he comes closer, and looks at the individual stones, beautiful in themselves, but, as he draws back again, he sees each one multiplied in beauty relative to the created image. The movement of this activity is a spiritual grace that leads directly to union with the Artist of the King's image.

Irenaeus's *Refutation and Overthrow of the Falsely Named Knowledge* serves as a monition for Christians everywhere, for there is nothing new under the sun. Just as those who are unfamiliar with Homer could be easily deceived by a clever reconstruction of his words, so are Christians ignorant of Scripture easy victims to modern narratives. On the other hand, those who become familiar with the Scriptures and the orthodox Tradition of right interpretation are safeguarded against those who forcibly prize the precious stones of Scripture from the established mosaic to reconstruct an inferior image foreign to the Gospel.

5. Conclusion

By way of conclusion, I return to Young's starting point, that watershed first principle of methodology, suspicion. Toward the end of her essay, Young evinces some reticence to live with the consequences of such methodological doubt. Postmodern herme-

---

49. Jerome, *Comm. Isa. Libri 18 libri 18 prol.: PL* 24, 17 B (quoted in the Second Vatican Council's Dogmatic Constitution on Divine Revelation, *Dei Verbum*, 25).

neutics, for all its promise, does not deliver the warm security she had hoped. What indeed about the truth of the matter?

> But there are ways in which pluralism and relativism ultimately undermine every claim to truth, and thus devalue all our researches along with any religious commitments we may have. It is not for nothing that there is so much talk of "play," for all we can do is "play" with texts, "play" with ideas, choosing the game we enjoy, joining the consumer society in the supermarket of life's options.[50]

And so, what criterion necessitates such a sweeping historical application of suspicion? Doubtless, "suspicion" yields original ideas, but suspicion in itself could be either rational or irrational. It is right to be suspicious of someone prone to lying or to treachery, for example. It is not good to be suspicious of people as an *a priori* principle. That would constitute paranoia. Suspicion as a methodological principle is not a realistic way to exist in the world, so why would this be the proper mode of historical methodology?

Something in particular makes patristic theology surprisingly *more vulnerable* than biblical theology, namely that while secular exegetes and historical critics of the Bible often—though certainly not always—show religious respect to their subject matter out of deference to the peoples who hold it sacred, secular scholars appear less inclined to extend a similar courtesy to the Fathers. Instead, they are icons to be smashed. What's more, it is good to do so, in the views of many researchers. As the narrative goes in some circles, these men escaped the world's notice for their alleged crimes for centuries until our more enlightened time. These men are the victors of their day, powerful authoritarians, and corrupt oppressors of minority Christian groups. Therefore, they are condemned without trial by iconoclastic historical revisionism. Or, at best, they are judged guilty in on the testimony of the few polemical witnesses whose works survive (Destroying the works of the ancient heretics—rather than being an act of charity for the spiritual good of their flocks—is further proof of the guilt of the Fathers). Because of the spread of scientific positivism, leading to a condi-

---

50. Young, "From Suspicion and Sociology to Spirituality," 432.

tion in the culture and in academia in which hypotheses and guesswork are confused with established fact, the polemical re-narrations of the *vitae patrum* make way for dogmatic pluralism. But if the weight of hagiographic evidence must be suspected, so too then must *cult* be, which in theory should not have arisen around these authoritarians had it not been imposed from without. The Fathers, after all, are not mere historical subjects but are venerated saints, one of the four criteria of patrology. Historical iconoclasm, therefore, cannot escape passing judgment upon the veneration *cultus*. But again, revisionists must provide a compelling case for a fabricated or illusory *cultus*.

Rather than quaffing the conclusions of historical revisionism uncritically, there remains much room to be suspicious of suspicion. One easily suspects suspicion for the crime of being a lousy methodological principle. But one must have good reasons *not* to be suspicious of the Fathers. Are they really to be exempted from the charges against them? I would certainly not advocate a broad eschewing of all critical scholarship that paints any of the Fathers in a negative light. Certainly, these men were sinners who made mistakes along the way. But a patrological method should in questionable matters extend the benefit of the doubt to them.

Fortunately, as with biblical theology, many theologians have devoted themselves not only to the task of expounding patristic doctrine but also to the task of engaging contemporary revisionism critically. In various ways, the Fathers stand in the way of false interpretations of Christian doctrine, and so their voice is vital not only to safeguard but also to echo down into every century. The patristic era is a central one theologically in the life of the church, in which the church was blessed with a select group of men whose lives were holy, set apart for the chief duty of passing along what they had received in a time of international expansion. They were not inventing, imagining, constructing, creating, in the sense that these notions are often understood, namely, of inventing something that was not there before, drawing a new reality out of phantasm, building something of their own making that resembled little of what went before, and giving existence to something that previously did not exist. Instead, they invented new ways to articulate what they already believed; they imagined by ridding their minds of images; they constructed creedal statements to lift the confusion of their flocks; and they created by participation in spreading the Gospel of Christ our God, who makes a new creature of each member of the newly baptized. It is as Khaled Anatolios said, concerning retrieving the classic theologies of patristics for the sake of the new evangelization: "We turn to them not with the assurance that they are infallible in every detail but simply with the recognition that they have proven to be built on the solid rock of the new terrain of the authentic Gospel."[51]

A theologian has a particular task, namely, that of passing along the faith to others. As shown above, patrology risks being obscured by certain trends predominating the study of Christianity in late antiquity, or early Christianity, or early christianities, or whatever new term or phrase shall arise. But, as Schmid argued,

> Patrology is of the highest importance for every student of theology. Theology is the science of revealed truth; but the two main sources of revealed truth are Scripture and tradition. Now the Fathers of the Church are the best expounders of the Holy Scripture, and they are also the chief witnesses and representatives of tradition. Hence it is plain that the study of the Fathers is absolutely necessary for the student of theology . . . No wonder, then, that the greatest theologians have ever applied themselves with the utmost diligence to the study of the holy Fathers.[52]

What are the ways forward to ensure that the study of the Fathers endures through this present iconoclasm? First of all, faculties of theology must pursue a right *ressourcement* in graduate education, called for by the late Fr. Matthew Lamb. In a survey he conducted at the time, he observed that 75 percent of doctoral theses focused upon figures from the twentieth century and an additional 15 percent focused on figures from the nineteenth century. Thus, only a tenth of doctoral theses were focusing upon the previous eighteen centuries, an unfitting tithe for the Catholic academy. For Lamb, the turn of the millennium constituted a new *kairos* for Catholic universities to reorient themselves toward a truly integral wisdom by returning to the sources:

---

51. Anatolios, "Patristic Reflection," 1071.
52. Schmid, *Manual of Patrology*, 20.

> There has been a definite "aggiornamento" in Catholic theology. What is needed now is that more attention be given to the "resourcement" so that, two decades hence, there might be more Catholic theologians with degrees in those important resources for Catholic the-ology: patristic, monastic, and medieval philosophers and theologians. This, I have tried to show, is more than a merely historical task. It is a question of attuning the minds and hearts of Catholic theologians to the Divine realities that would assure real, and not merely notional, apprehension and assent in theology.[53]

While it would be a worthwhile endeavor, it is beyond my immediate personal resources to replicate Lamb's survey and look at the past three decades. Lamb's call should still be heard, namely, that there needs to be a bigger tent of theologians devoted to the study of *sacra doctrina* as articulated by the Fathers in order to pass along their wisdom.

Secondly, because contemporary hermeneutical approaches to the Fathers are so deeply indebted to the principles of the historical-critical method, it is a fitting time for a vigorous appropriation of the effective modes of "criticism of criticism" that have come out of biblical scholarship in recent decades. Such an endeavor would be unsuccessful if it degenerated merely into patristic apologetics. Conversely, it would be successful if it met specious hermeneutical frameworks on their own philosophical turf. Before beginning the act of reading, scholars have adopted as their own logical propositions and epistemological assertions that affect their ability to connect with ancient texts. Those propositions—history is utterly inaccessible, modes of social oppression were inscribed into ancient works, ancient words fail to communicate meaning, the power or motives of ancient writers make them untrustworthy, present-day modes of reading are more valuable than the original mode of writing, etc.—should be addressed on philosophical grounds. Such propositions inform a certain mode of historical research, but at their core those propositions are epistemological and have to do with truth claims. This present essay has attempted to venture down that path, but there remains so very much to do.

---

53. Lamb, "Challenges," 128.

Thirdly, patristic theologians should resist the temptation to seclude themselves to some theological island paradise and muse on divine truths while ignoring the polemical works coming from the revisionist history of late antiquity. Instead, it is better to "suffer divine things" with the Fathers and to contemplate the wisdom in their work *while also* making bold to engage works built upon "suspicion of received accounts." One of the most important things patristic theologians should do, in my view, is to show up and collaborate. There are many excellent historians of late antiquity who appreciate patrology or who at least are not hostile to it. Whether from a piety arising out of their own confession or from a sincere appreciation of the Fathers, they too do not wish to see their objects of study dashed to irrelevance. Some teach history or civilization courses in universities who are attempting to build the kingdom of Christ *by teaching authentic history*. Such individuals can very much help to enrich one's understanding of the age of the Fathers. Moreover, there is no good in being insular. A patrologist has the need to make historical claims freely about the lives and writings of the Fathers. While the primary focus must remain on the Tradition, it is impossible to study the Fathers and not to be a historian. While those who have focused their studies on theology have much to learn from historians about historical methodology, interdisciplinary openness enlarges both history and theology. When "patristics" journals and associations lose interest in rigorous theology as "too confessional" and forget the importance of pursuing truth, they stand as gatekeepers in the way of the interdisciplinary enlargement of both history and theology. Even as new associations and new publication venues arise in light of the vast interest in patristic theology among Catholics, Orthodox, and Protestants, it is important for social historians to reject an insularity that hinders their own engagement with confessional scholars, many of whom are eminent historians in their own right.

Indeed, one of the barriers to be overcome is a bit of a construct itself, and that is the notion of *historical theology* as a separate discipline from theology itself. Joseph Lienhard brought forth the difficulties in this term, in that (a) either it means something of an umbrella term for all things having to do with Christian history, whether the history of dogma, heresy, the church, Christian thought, etc.; or (b) or it means something like what Jaroslav Pelikan described as "the genetic study of Christian faith and doctrine."[54] The difficulty in the ambiguity—though there is clearly something of an advantage to be detected as well—is this:

> The historical theologian can see himself primarily as a historian, or primarily as a theologian. If he sees himself as a historian, his subject matter is the history of Christian thought, ideas, and perhaps institutions, and he uses the ordinary methods of historical science. He will often assert his objectivity, and assure his readers that faith does not interfere with his scholarly pursuits. If he sees himself primarily as a theologian, then his task is more delicate. He lives with the ambiguity of joining the terms "history" and "theology," the one dealing with the singular in space and time, the other with the Absolute beyond space and time, and seeks to balance the scholarly norms of historical science with the commitment of a believing theologian.[55]

Historical theologians face a built-in pressure to determine their direction. At the same time, a historian should be careful not to presuppose that the God over history cannot act within it, as Immanuel Kant did, in his exaltation of the pure religion of reason over that of historical faith, which he argues cannot in any sense be universal. Historical theology's approach to the object of its study "does not mine the past out of an antiquated curiosity or to confirm a modern thesis," Lienhard argues. Instead, it "attempts, first of all, to read and understand the Christian writing of the past in their own context, for all they have to offer, and then to discern the growth in understanding of God's definitive self-revelation in Christ across the centuries, as it is worked out in the interpretation of Scripture, in the Church's teaching, in the liturgy, and in theology."[56]

---

54. Lienhard, "Historical Theology," 270; cf. Pelikan, *Historical Theology*, xiii; Daley, "Historical Theology." On the difficulty that the discipline of history faces before the challenges posed by an increased despair to derive meaning from historical texts and by postmodern historians who prioritize the reading subject in the historical science, see Evans, *In Defense of History*.

55. Lienhard, "Historical Theology," 270–71.

56. Lienhard, "Historical Theology," 271. He cites *Murder in the Cathedral*, bringing forth T. S. Eliot's understanding of the risk of loss in the historical quest. Lienhard writes, "The Tempter says to Thomas Becket:

Why can we not simply cast aside the Fathers, or, worse, castrate "early Christianity" of its "maleness" in order to make it more palatable to modern sentiments? Well, if we rid ourselves of the ones the church has long recognized as the authentic interpreters of Sacred Scripture, then we are left with new authorities to lead us to the "proper" readings of Scripture. In the words of Kant, "under this system, historical faith must finally become mere faith in scriptural scholars and their insight."[57] An oracle of doom indeed! John Paul II, however, answers the Kantian objection of the impossibility of God's breaking into a historical moment:

> The word of God is not addressed to any one people or to any one period of history. Similarly, dogmatic statements, while reflecting at times the culture of the period in which they were defined, formulate an unchanging and ultimate truth . . . Human language may be conditioned by history and constricted in other ways, but the human being can still express truths which surpass the phenomenon of language. Truth can never be confined to time and culture; in history it is known, but it also reaches beyond history.[58]

Finally, I wish to end on a pedagogical note. Returning to the sources brings much profit to the classroom discussion and edifies students' faith. I have often read excerpts of the works of the Fathers with my students, who are mostly Catholic seminarians, in the classroom. The Fathers' power to elucidate *sacra doctrina* remains ever fresh. At the same time, encountering wisdom in the sources smashes our historical hubris, that we know everything better simply because we own the present. Careful confessional scholars, whether they are more inclined toward patrology or toward the more historical concerns, must have a voice. It is good

---

And later is worse, when men will not hate you
Enough to defame or to execrate you,
But pondering the qualities that you lacked
Will only try to find the historical fact.
When men shall declare that there was no mystery
About this man who played a certain part in history."
57. Kant, *Religion*, 105.
58. John Paul II, *Fides et Ratio*, 95.

for patristics broadly and in everyone's best interests that patristics not become the primary possession of popular apologists, who often reduce the Fathers to authenticators of their own arguments. Instead, the Fathers are valuable precisely as fonts of wisdom, instructors in the *sapiential mode of theology*, which is why the expansion of patristics and a return to their thought has such promise. Lamb notes the transformative power this *ressourcement* would have upon modern culture. "A recovery of Catholic intellectual memories will enlighten our postmodern world, offering new possibilities of creating cultures capable of properly relating wisdom and science, tradition and innovation, the university and the Church."[59]

Thomas Aquinas prayed before study *Da mihi . . . interpretandi subtilitatem*. Correct interpretation is never a given. Christian scholars broadly—Catholic, Orthodox, and Protestant—believe that the Holy Spirit led the Fathers to illumine the Scriptures and has guided the church throughout the course of history. That means that the subjects of our study are those who in pursuit of the divine life "suffered divine things," to borrow again from Dionysius. The four characteristics of a Father—orthodoxy, sanctity, antiquity, approval by the church—work in tandem to give us a group of generally trustworthy authorities. Life in the Spirit (sanctity) led them to right teaching (orthodoxy) in the earliest days of Christianity (antiquity) which led later generations of Christians to put them forward as wise guides of theology (approval by the church). Thus, their claims about God and Christ cannot simply be set side-by-side with those of any ancient author. In that light, interpretation is best assured when reading the Fathers in the Spirit in which they wrote, in a spirit of prayer recognizing them to be trustworthy guides. It is my hope that in our continuing to make the Fathers accessible to readers, these luminaries may always have the opportunity to make clear the Scriptures, awakening the faith of the person who stumbles upon them. Their minds were fixed upon the Holy Trinity and upon the figure of Jesus Christ, especially the mysteries of his Incarnation and salvific economy. Patrological work is a success proportionate to the

---

59. Lamb, "Challenges," 120.

extent that it helps facilitate that encounter with this mind-set of the Fathers. To lose such a mind-set is truly the loss of patrology itself, that is, patristic theology.

Bibliography

Anatolios, Khaled. "A Patristic Reflection on the Nature and Method of Theology in the New Evangelization." *Nova et Vetera* 14 (2016) 1067–81.

Bauer, Walter *Orthodoxy and Heresy in Earliest Christianity*, edited by Robert A. Kraft and Gerhard Krodel. Translated by Philadelphia Seminar on Christian Origins. Mifflintown, PA: Sigler, 1996.

Benedict XVI. "Biblical Interpretation in Conflict." In *God's Word: Scripture—Tradition—Office*, edited by Peter Hünermann and Thomas Söding. Translated by Henry Taylor, 91–126. San Francisco: Ignatius, 2008.

Bock, Darrell. *The Missing Gospels: Unearthing the Truth behind Alternative Christianities*. Nashville: Nelson, 2006.

Brakke, David. "Self-Differentiation among Christian Groups: The Gnostics and Their Opponents." In *Cambridge History of Christianity: Volume 1. Origins to Constantine*, edited by Margaret M. Mitchell and Frances M. Young, 245–60. Cambridge: Cambridge University Press, 2014.

Brock, Sebastian P., and Susan Ashbrook Harvey. *Holy Women of the Syrian Orient*. Transformation of Classical Heritage 13. Berkeley: University of California Press, 1998.

Cameron, Averil. "The Cost of Orthodoxy." *Church History and Religious Culture* 93 (2013) 339–61.

Clark, Elizabeth A. "From Patristics to Early Christian Studies." *Oxford Handbook of Early Christian Studies*, edited by

Susan Ashbrook Harvey and David G. Hunter, 7–41. Oxford: Oxford University Press, 2008.

———. *History, Theory, Text: Historians and the Linguistic Turn*. Cambridge, MA: Harvard University Press, 2004.

Cohick, Lynn H., and Amy Brown Hughes. *Christian Women in the Patristic World: Their Influence, Authority, and Legacy in the Second through Fifth Centuries*. Grand Rapids: Baker Academic, 2017.

Daley, Brian E. "Historical Theology Today and Tomorrow." In *Religion, Scholarship, and Higher Education: Perspectives, Models, and Future Prospects*, edited by Andrea Sterk, 117–27. Notre Dame, IN: University of Notre Dame Press, 2002.

Drobner, Hubertus R. *The Fathers of the Church: A Comprehensive Introduction*. Translated by Siegfried S. Schatzmann. Grand Rapids: Baker Academic, 2007.

Ehrman, Bart, and Andrew Jacobs, eds. *Christianity in Late Antiquity: 300–450 C.E.: A Reader*. New York: Oxford University Press, 2004.

Evans, Richard J. *In Defense of History*. New York: Norton, 1999.

Henry, Patrick. "Why Is Contemporary Scholarship So Enamored of Ancient Heretics?" *Studia Patristica* 17 (1982) 123–26.

John Paul II. Encyclical Letter. *Fides et Ratio*. September 14, 1998.

Jurgens, William A. *The Faith of the Early Fathers: Volume 1*. Collegeville, MN: Liturgical, 1970.

Kannengiesser, Charles. "The Future of Patristics." *Theological Studies* 52 (1991) 128–39.

Kant, Immanuel. *Religion within the Limits of Reason Alone*. Translated by Theodore M. Greene and Hoyt H. Hudson. New York: Harper, 1960.

King, Karen "Which Early Christianity?" *Oxford Handbook of Early Christian Studies*, edited by Susan Ashbrook Harvey and David G. Hunter, 66–84. Oxford: Oxford University Press, 2008.

Köstenberger, Andreas J., and Michael J. Kruger. *The Heresy of Orthodoxy: How Contemporary Culture's Fascination with Diversity Has Reshaped our Understanding of Early Christianity*. Wheaton, IL: Crossway, 2010.

Lamb, Matthew L. "Challenges for Catholic Graduate Theological Education." In *Theological Education in the Catholic Tradition: Contemporary Challenges*, edited by Patrick W. Carey and Earl C. Muller, 108–30. New York: Crossroad, 1997.

Lienhard, Joseph T. "Historical Theology in the Curriculum." In *Theological Education in the Catholic Tradition: Contemporary Challenges*, edited by Patrick W. Carey and Earl C. Muller, 266–79. New York: Crossroad, 1997.

Lieu, Judith. *Marcion and the Making of a Heretic: God and Scripture in the Second Century*. New York: Cambridge University Press, 2015.

Miller, Patricia Cox, ed. *Women in Early Christianity: Translations from Greek Texts*. Washington, DC: Catholic University of America Press, 2005.

O'Neill, Taylor Patrick. "The Primacy of the Speculative in the Science of Theology: Editorial Essay." *Lux Veritatis: A Journal of Speculative Theology* 1 (2024) 2–14.

O'Regan, Cyril. *Gnostic Return in Modernity*. Albany, NY: State University of New York Press, 2001.

Pelikan, Jaroslav. *Historical Theology: Continuity and Change in Christian Doctrine*. New York: Corpus, 1971.

Schmid, Bernard. *Manual of Patrology*. 2nd ed. St. Louis: B. Herder, 1903.

Tixeront, J. *A Handbook of Patrology*. Translated by S. A. Raemers. 5th ed. St. Louis: B. Herder, 1934.

United States Conference of Catholic Bishops. *Program of Priestly Formation in the United States of America*. 6th ed. Washington, DC: US Conference of Catholic Bishops, 2022.

Vinzent, Markus. *Marcion and the Dating of the Synoptic Gospels*. Studia Patristica Supplement 2. Leuven: Peeters, 2014.

Young, Frances. "From Suspicion and Sociology to Spirituality: On Method, Hermeneutics and Appropriation with Respect to Patristic Material." *Studia Patristica* 29 (1997) 421–35.

HERMENEUTICS IN AUGUSTINE'S DE DOCTRINA CHRISTIANA
BOOKS TWO AND THREE[1]

Tarmo Toom
Tartu University, Tartu, Estonia

De doctrina Christiana is among the first treatises that Augustine penned as a bishop (396 CE) although he did not finish it at that time. This treatise is about many things, but preeminently it is about interpreting Scripture. It is written for those who look for "real understanding and careful investigation of their meaning" (*bene intellegendis et diligenter earum sensibus indagandis*) (4.5.7).[2]

De doctrina Christiana begins with a programmatic statement: "There are certain rules for interpreting the scriptures ... It is my intention to communicate these [rules] (*Sunt praecepta quaedam tractandarum scripturarum . . . Haec tradere institui*)" (*Prol.* 1.1).[3] In doing so, Augustine divides his treatise into two major parts: "There are two things on which all interpretation of Scrip-

---

1. This article is written with the help of the Estonian Research Council (ETAG) grant STP4 "Patristic Introductions (*introductiones*) to the Bible and its Interpretation."
2. Augustine, *De Doctrina Christiana*, 202–3. Babcock assesses, "Certain portions of the work tempt us into supposing that [Augustine] is delineating [various programs]. Such interpretations, however, seem to extend their reach far beyond their grasp, taking smaller components within the work as if they set the program for the whole" ("*Caritas* and Signification," 145).
3. Unlike Schleiermacher who insisted that there was no special hermeneutics for Scripture although its content was unique (Schleiermacher, *Hermeneutics and Criticism*, 15), Augustine's advice was accompanied with a conditional clause which limited his endeavor to a particular case: "As far as the books of holy Scripture are concerned" (*quantum ad libros divinarum scripturarum spectat*) (*Doctr. chr.* 3.4.8); cf. Andrews, *Hermeneutics and the Church*, 71–115.

ture depends: the process of discovering what we need to learn, and the process of presenting what we have learnt" (*Duae sunt res quibus nititur omnis tractatio scripturarum, modus inveniendi quae intelligenda sunt et modus proferendi quae intellecta sunt*) (1.1.1; cf. 4.1.1). Accordingly, the macro-structure of *De doctrina Christiana* consists of the aspect of discovery (*modus inveniendi*), which corresponds to the first three books of *De doctrina Christiana*, and of the aspect of presenting (*modus proferendi*), which corresponds to Book Four. The *modus inveniendi* portion of the treatise, in turn, consists of the subject-matter that Scripture addresses and the resources it uses for doing so. This means that Book One is predominantly about the subject-matter (*res*) of Scripture, and Books Two and Three about the ways in which words (*signa*) refer to this subject-matter.[4] As Augustine puts it, "All teaching is teaching of either things or signs" (*Omnis doctrina vel rerum est vel signorum*) (1.2.2; cf. 2.1.1).[5]

Cassiodorus famously identified the most important patristic treatises on biblical interpretation which were available for Latin readers and named them *introductiones* (*Inst.* 1.10). Among these, he mentioned Augustine's *De doctrina Christiana*, which is the first known work that employs semiotics for biblical interpreta-

---

4. The reason for such a sequence of topics is epistemological: "A sign is learned when the thing is known, rather than the thing being learned when the sign is given" (*magis signum re cognita quam signo dato ipsa res discitur*) (*Mag.* 10.33). Words as referential signs make sense only when that which they point to is known. Accordingly, Book One is about "the things which are objects of our faith" (*de rebus continentibus fidem*) (*Doctr. chr.* 1.40.44), including both the *regula fidei* (1.5.5–1.21.19 [cf. Istace, "Le livre," 297–98]) and *regula dilectionis* or the double commandment of love (1.26.27–1.30.33; 1.35.39–1.36.41; 1.40.44 [cf. Matt 22:37–40; Sieben, "Die 'res' der Bibel," 72–80]).
5. Both Cicero and Quintilian taught that speech as such consisted of that which was signified (i.e., the subject-matter or *res*) and that which signified (i.e., the expressive form or *verba*) (Cicero, *Or.* 3.5.19; Quintilian, *Inst.* 3.3.1, 3.5.1; cf. Augustine, *Acad.* 2.11.25).

tion.⁶ The result is an astounding *scientia signorum*.⁷ This *scientia* is primarily about signification, but it aslo includes various disussions of other hermeneutical matters. These hermeneutical matters cannot be isolated from Augustine's overall discussion of signs and signification, but they can be highlighted without always discussing signification per se.

Accordingly, the goal of this article is to identify and assess the hermeneutical topics that Augustine has decided to examine in Books Two and Three in order to be able to compare these, in another time, with those found in other *introductiones*.⁸ All this, in turn, would enable one to figure out what the Latin patristic hermeneutical advice amounted to when medieval authors started to follow Cassiodorus' recommendation.

Book Two

In Book Two of *De doctrina Christiana*, Augustine's aim is to "examine and discuss" (*considerare atque tractare*) signa data, the intentionally given conventional word-signs. As word-signs both veil and reveal the intentions of speaker/writer, the veiling aspect (*obtegere*) has two main causes: the signs are either "unknown" (*ignota*) or "ambiguous" (*ambigua*). Both groups are divided further into literal (*propria*) and figurative (*translata*) signs (2.10.15; 2.14.21).

In the case of Scripture, however, the *signa data* that Augustine focuses on have to be taken as mediated *signa divinitus data* (2.2.3). Augustine explains that words in Scripture communicate

---

6. Augustine hardly presents a full-blown theory signification. Instead, what he provides is a set of resources for it (see King, "Augustine on Language," 299; cf. Cameron, *Christ Meets Me Everywhere*, 239).

7. Bochet and Madec, "Les signes"; Borsche, "Zeichentheorie im Übergang"; Cary, *Outward Signs*; Gramigna, *Augustine's Theory*; Jackson, "Semantics and Hermeneutics," 87–152; Manetti, *Theories of the Sign*, 157–68; Markus, "St. Augustine on Signs"; Toom, "Augustine's Hermeneutics."

8. A comparative chart of thirty-three hermeneutical topics identified in the *introductiones* can be found in Toom, "Ancient Christian Textbooks."

"the thoughts and wishes of those by whom it was written down and, through them, the will of God" (*quam cogitationes voluntatemque illorum a quibus conscripta est invenire et per illas voluntatem dei*) (2.5.6; cf. 3.9.13).[9] In order to communicate,[10] these two sets of intentions—human and divine—make use of languages which are finite, ever-changing, imprecise, and ambiguous. The result is texts which need to be interpreted in order to discover the intended meaning(s) of these signs as the means of communication.[11] Hence, the necessity of hermeneutics.

In addition to the complication that God's will is mediated through human agents, Scripture has circulated "far and wide in the various languages of translation" (*per varias interpretum linguas longe lateque diffusa*) (2.5.6). Consequently, readers can easily "be misled by obscurities and ambiguities of many kinds" (*Sed multis et multiplicibus obscuritatibus et ambiguitatibus decipiuntur*) (2.6.7 [translation modified]).[12] Perhaps the Holy Spirit intended it so, because the joy of discovery after hard work is always sweeter than gaining results without any effort (2.6.7–8; cf. 4.6.9; 4.8.22).[13] Augustine conceals some of his hermeneutical advice already in his deliberation about the sweet pleasure of unlocking textual conundrums. It says that virtually all the obscure passages can be understood with help of "plainer passages" (*locis*

---

9. Cf. Augustine, *Enarrat. Ps.* 104.27.

10. Augustine is interested in *signa data* as in communicative signs (King, "Augustine on Language," 292–300).

11. To use a Stoic distinction (Diogenes Laertius, *Vit.* 7.57), the interpreter's task is to perceive the words on a page and their grammatical use (*lexis*) as a meaningful discourse (*logos*), to perceive the signified with the help of signifiers. James calls such required mental operation of an interpreter a movement "from *lexis* to *logos*" (*Learning the Language of Scripture*, 73–112). Gregory the Great compared those, who were foolishly satisfied with the mere "letter," to a person who sees only the colors of a picture and not the picture itself (*Exp. CC.* 1.4).

12. Cf. Augustine, *Dial.* 8; Cicero, *Inv.* 1.15.20–21; Quintilian, *Inst.* 7.5.6. The distinction that Augustine makes between obscurity (*obscuritas*) and ambiguity (*ambiguitas*) corresponds largely to the distinction between unknown signs (*Doctr. chr.* 2) and ambiguous signs (*Doctr. chr.* 3).

13. Cf. Augustine, *Enarrat. Ps.* 46.1; 149.14; *ep.* 55.11.21.

apertioribus) (2.6.8).[14] This is a topic that he will pick up again in 2.9.14.

The fact that Augustine's hermeneutical advice proper does not begin with a set of clever rules and sophisticated instructions, but by insisting on the moral and spiritual prerequisites of the interpreter of Scripture is significant. As Augustine says elsewhere, "Whoever fancies he can have an insight into truth, while he is yet living a wicked life, is mistaken" (*Errat autem quisquis putat ueritatem se posse cognoscere, cum adhuc nequiter uiuat*).[15] In *De doctrina Christiana*, he intertwines a rearranged scriptural passage (Isa 11:2–3 [LXX]) with a Platonic idea of conversion from temporal and sensible to eternal and intelligible, and postulates a seven-step "ladder."[16] The reason for mentioning moral prerequisites before anything else is scriptural: "The fear of the Lord is the beginning of wisdom" (Prov 9:10 cited in *Doctr. chr.* 2.7.11).

After considering the moral and spiritual requirements for being an apt interpreter of Scripture, Augustine determines the hermeneutical object; that is, he determines the books through which God's will is believed to be communicated (2.9.14). This hermeneutical object is the canonical (*canonicae*) Scripture. The first requirement is to "read them all" (*totas legerit*) (2.8.12). But what does "all" mean?

Augustine is fully aware of the fact that there is no absolute consensus in the larger church about the canon, but he appeals to the consensus established by the more prominent churches and the understanding of the majority of churches. In *Doctr. chr.* 2.8.13, he lists the "complete" (*totus*) canon of Scripture, which consists of forty-four books of the Old Testament, plus the twenty-seven books of the New Testament.[17] Augustine evidently never had in

---

14. In *Enarrat. Ps.* 10.8, Augustine compares the obscure and plain passages to God's eyelids which are respectively either closed or open.

15. Augustine, *Agon.* 13.14.

16. Cf. Augustine, *Serm. Dom.* 1.1.1–5.15. In addition to *De doctrina Christiana*, van Lierde mentions twenty-two other texts of Augustine which discuss Isa 11:2–3 (van Lierde, "Teaching of St. Augustine," 7–13). See also Kamimura, "Augustine's Scriptural Exegesis."

17. Cf. Augustine, *Civ.* 15.23; la Bonnardière, "Le canon." Except the order of some books, Augustine's canon matches with that of the

his possession a one-volume codex of the whole bible, including both the Old and the New Testament, for pandects were very rare, but he nevertheless had a pretty good idea what the "complete" Bible should look like. To get the number forty-four, Augustine has to count all the Old Testament books found in the Septuagint,[18] to count individually all the minor prophets,[19] and expand the book of Jeremiah to include Lamentations, Baruch, and the Epistle of Jeremiah.[20] The two books of Ezra are probably not Ezra and Nehemiah, but more likely Esdras A and Esdras B of the Greek tradition.[21] In his list of the New Testament books, the positioning of Colossians, James, and the book of Acts differ from what is common in western Christianity today.[22] Interestingly, the positioning of James and the book of Acts does not match with the order of books that can found in Augustine's *De scriptura sancta speculum*. [23]

While speaking about the canonical Scripture, a particular hermeneutical feature that Augustine highlights (again) is that plainer passages teach "all the things" (*omnia*) that concern faith

---

Breviarium Hipponense (Gallagher and Meade, *Biblical Canon Lists*, 222–30; Munier, "La tradition manuscrite"). In *Inst*. 1.13, Cassiodorus gives a report on Augustine's canon and modifies it by placing the two books of Esdras before Maccabees, and Major Prophets before Minor Prophets (O'Loughlin, "Structure").

18. The Septuagint as such had different contents and arrangements. Therefore, to say that Augustine followed the canon of the LXX means that he included other books than those which could be found in the Jewish canon (Lange, "History")

19. This is the case despite Augustine saying that these books "are joined together and never separated" (*qui conexi sibimet, quoniam numquam seiuncti sunt*) and should thus be counted as one (*Doctr. chr.* 2.8.13).

20. Gallagher and Meade, *Biblical Canon Lists*, 225.

21. Bogaert, "Les livres d'Esdras," 12–13.

22. A mid-fourth-century Cheltenham Canon, the provenance of which is from Africa, gives a different order to the four gospels, as well as omits Hebrews, James, and Jude (Gallagher and Meade, *Biblical Canon Lists*, 188–93).

23. *De scriptura sancta speculum*, if authentic, was written after 427 and it is an anthology of biblical passages in the canonical order of books.

and morality and thus, facilitate the understanding of the more obscure passages (2.9.14; cf. 3.2.2). He presumed that the texts in the canonical Scripture formed a coherent whole.[24] As Augustine put it elsewhere, Scripture is the "one single utterance of God" (*unus sermo Dei*).[25] This "single utterance" cannot be self-contradictory and thus, an exegete has to look for such interpretations of particular passages which would cohere with the other passages in the Bible.[26] Augustine also wisely remarks that, in order that these other passages might illuminate a given passage, Scripture has to be memorized as much as possible.[27]

Among the remedies for ascertaining the unknown literal *signa data*, Augustine recommends the "knowledge of languages" (*linguarum cognitio*) (2.11.16; 2.13.19; 2.14.21). In order to understand Scripture adequately, readers of the Latin Bible—i.e., of a translation—should consult the texts in Hebrew and Greek.[28] Particularly because there is an "infinite variety of Latin translations" (*latinorum interpretum infinita varietas*),[29] checking the "earlier versions" (*ad exemplaria praecedentia*) is strongly recommended (2.11.16 [translation modified]).[30]

---

24. Augustine, *Civ.* 18.43; *Gen. litt.* 5.8.23; *Tract. Ev. Jo.* 19.7; Schultheiß, "Augustinus," 60.

25. Augustine, *Enarrat. Ps.* 103.4.1.

26. Cf. Augustine, *Tract. Ev. Jo.* 16.4.

27. It seems though that Augustine himself had not memorized the whole Scripture, for at least at times he needed his codices in order to recite Scripture (*s.* 23.19 [Dolbeau]).

28. Schirner, *Inspice*, 24–45. Good examples of Augustine consulting the Greek text can be found in *Enarrat. Ps.* 50.19; 67.7, 24, 41; 71.8; 77.42; 78.17; 104.3, 6, 14–15; 105.2, 5; 118.11.6; 118.17.1; *ep.* 261.5; *Gen. litt.* 7.1.2; *Tract. Ev. Jo.* 2.14; 104.3.

29. Cf. Augustine, *ep.* 71.4.6; Houghton, "Earliest Latin Translations"; Schulz-Flügel, "Der lateinische Bibeltext," 110–11. Augustine's remark about everyone attempting to make his or her own Latin translation seems to be a rhetorical exaggeration since it does not fit well with the manuscript evidence.

30. Green supplies here the word "original," but obviously no original texts of Scripture, either in Greek or Hebrew, were available. In *Enarrat. Ps.* 38.2 (cf. 118.14.2), Augustine says, "The earlier language clarifies the one that came later" (*exponit sequentem lingua praecedens*).

However, the existence of the "variety of Latin translations" should not be taken as a mere hindrance, because one can also compare various translations and get a better sense of what the obscure texts might mean (2.12.17; 2.14.21).[31] Still, the ideal of consulting texts in Hebrew and Greek is beneficial, despite the fact that these languages—like any other language—are ambiguous as well.[32] Because texts as such are ambiguous, translators "may import a meaning which is quite unrelated to the writer's meaning" (*et eam significationem transfert quae a sensu scriptoris penitus aliena est*) (2.12.18). And worse still, if translators happen to come up with that which is "plain wrong" (*falsa*), then such translations need to be corrected (2.12.18; 2.14.21).[33] Thus, before attempting to interpret Scripture, its correct text, or at least the best text possible, has to be determined.

Speaking about the available translations, Augustine recommends a type of text which he calls *Itala* (vis-à-vis *Afra*), "for it keeps more closely to the words without sacrificing clarity of expression" (*nam est verborum tenacior cum perspicuitate sententia*) (2.15.22).[34] Arguably he means some early Latin versions which were known in Northern Italy (including Milan), and some of which he might have brought with him when he returned to Africa.[35] Yet, even such manuscripts as those of *Itala* should be compared with the Septuagint (rather than with any of the Hebrew

---

31. In *Doctr. chr.* 2.14.21, Green translates "to collect (*collatio*) manuscripts," but since Augustine is talking about comparing manuscripts, it would be better to have "to collate manuscripts."

32. Augustine agrees with a dialectician Chrysippus who said, "Every word is ambiguous" (*ambiguum esse omne verbum*) (cited in Augustine, *Dial.* 9 [Jackson, *Augustine: De dialectica*, 106–7) and therefore, he appraises ambiguity not as a vice of style but rather as an inherent problem of language as such (Jackson, *Augustine: De dialectica*, 106–7).

33. For *emendatio*, see Cassiodorus, *Inst.* 1.15.

34. Bochet and Madec, "Le Canon des Écritures," 521–22; Schirner, *Inspice*, 39–41, 46–53; Schildenberger, "Itala des heiligen Augustinus," 100–102.

35. Bogaert, "Les bibles d'Augustin," 521–23.

versions[36]) and corrected, if needed (2.15.22).[37] The reason is that "the authority of the Septuagint is supreme" (*septuaginta . . . excellit auctoritas*) (2.15.22). Therefore, even if the Hebrew text at times says something different,[38] God has provided a "fuller meaning" through this unanimous inspired translation (2.15.22).[39] Augustine is adamant: "it would not be right to any one person, however expert" (*ne sic quidem quemquam unum hominem qualibet peritia*) to correct the work of the seventy (2.15.22).[40]

Another thing in connection with the unknown literal *signa data* that Augustine emphasizes is the need to pay careful attention to the immediate literary context of words. He states the importance of considering the literary context twice (the end of 2.12.18 and the end of 2.13.20). He also repeats his corresponding hermeneutical advice yet again: the meaning of an expression can "become clear from the passages which precede and follow it, or both" (*vel talis lectio quae vel praecedentibus vel consequentibus vel utrisque ostendat*) (2.14.21).[41] The point is "semantic holism,"

---

36. Before the activity of Jerome, there is no evidence of Latin translations being based on the Hebrew *Vorlage* (Houghton, "Earliest Latin Translations," 2–3).

37. Reíllo, "Latin Bible," 19–22; Schirner, *Inspice*, 43–44. Even in the case of the text which were originally written in Hebrew (e.g., Genesis or Psalms), Augustine almost always corrects the Latin readings with the Greek Septuagint.

38. Cf. Augustine, *Civ.* 15.14, 23; 17.20; 18.26; *Cons.* 2.66.128; *Doctr. chr.* 4.7.15.

39. Cf. Augustine, *Civ.* 18.42-43; *Enarrat. Ps.* 135.3. In *De doctrina Christiana* and elsewhere as well, Augustine accepts Aristeas's famous account of the translation of the Septuagint. For how the Septuagint can give the "fuller meaning," see Toom, "Babel."

40. Cf. Augustine, *Civ.* 18.43; *Enarrat. Ps.* 28.2.2. The phrase "one person" can refer either to Jerome(!), Aquila, Symmachus, or Theodotion.

41. In the case of ambiguous words, this advice is repeated in *Doctr. chr.* 3.2.2–3.3.6; 3.25.37. Already in *Dial.* 9, Augustine contended that an ambiguous word was "made clear (*clarescat*) by a statement in which it occurs," and in *Doctr. chr.* 2.12.18, he demonstrates how the correct meaning of a Greek word *moscheumata* "is revealed in the words that follow" (*clarescit consequentibus verbis*). Contextual disambiguation is also recommended by Cicero, *Inv.* 2.40.117 and Quintilian, *Inst.* 7.9.7.

which means that while words taken individually and in isolation can mean all kind of things, then occurring in a sentence or a paragraph, their meaning is restricted by their actual use and context.[42]

Moving on to the next group of word-signs, to one's handling of unknown figurative (*translata*) signs in 2.16.23, Augustine has already explained that signs are figurative "when the actual things which we signify by the particular words are used to signify something else" (*cum et ipsae res quas propriis verbis significamus, ad aliquid aliud significandum usurpantur*) (2.10.15; cf. 1.2.2).[43] This means that next to knowledge of languages, knowledge of things (*rerum*) proves necessary as well. Because of the possible second level signification of things, various "hidden" (*secretum*) meanings of scriptural statements are possible (2.16.23). And here Augustine launches a major excursus on the usefulness of "secular" learning (2.16.24–2.42.63; cf. 3.29.40). Although there was no consensus about the legitimacy of using "secular" studies for interpreting Scripture among patristic authors, Augustine recommended these highly.[44] The reason is that knowledge of things enabled one to recognize the features of various things that Scripture employs for the sake of "some analogy" (*similitudinis alicuius*) (2.16.24; cf. 2.25.38).[45] The examples he discusses include snakes, stones, herbs, carbuncle, olive branch, hyssop, and after that, numbers and music (2.16.24–2.18.28).

---

42. King, "Augustine on Language," 304–5; cf. Wittgenstein, *Philosophical Investigations*, §43 and §432. James distinguishes between the "semantic aspect" of a sentence, which has a meaning "irrespective of its context of use," and the "pragmatic aspect," which "depends on its use in a particular speech situation" (*Learning the Language of Scripture*, 114).

43. In *Doctr. chr.* 3.9.13, Augustine calls a thing which signified another thing *res significans*.

44. Some authors, such as Cassiodorus, *Inst.* 2; esp. 1.28.4; 2.3.22; 2.7.4; *Concl.* 3; Origen (*Ep. Greg.* 1), Adrian (*Isag.* 75–76), Junillus (*Inst.* Preface) encouraged it, Tyconius (*Reg.* 4), Cassian (*Inst.* 5.34), and Gregory the Great (*Moral.* 5) did not (see Pollmann, "Re-Appropriation").

45. Cf. Augustine, *Gen. imp.* 14.45; Tyconius, *Reg.* 6.3.1.26; 6.3.2.39–40.

Before continuing with his interpretative advice, Augustine gives a forewarning. He distinguishes between things that humans establish or institute (*instituere*), and the things that humans simply observe (*animadvertere*) (2.19.29). The first group consists of idol-worship, magic, amulets, astrology, and other such superstitious phenomena (2.20.30–31). Augustine makes clear that, by use of *res* in a figurative sense, he does not have superstitious divinations in mind which is indeed a "great mistake and great folly" (*magnus error et magna dementia*) (2.22.33). These are but mere conventions established with demons (2.22.33; 2.24.37; 2.26.40).[46] Christians must "totally reject and avoid" (*repudianda et fugienda*) such "knowledge" (2.23.36).

During this a bit drawn-out excursus, Augustine brings up the notion of "convention/agreement" (*consensio*) several times (2.24.37–2.25.38). He contends that the relation between a name and the thing it names is arbitrary and a matter of agreement which is established in various linguistic communities. Thus, in this issue of language being either natural or conventional, Augustine sides with Aristotle (conventional), rather than with Stoics (natural).[47] Because language is conventional, word-signs can be "correct" even in their multi-referential use.[48] Although Augustine admits that knowledge of the etymology of names can be useful, language as such is still primarily conventional.[49] This matters for

46. Markus, *Signs and Meanings*, 125–46.
47. In *Int.* 16a20, Aristotle states that "a noun is a sound having meaning established by convention (*kata synthēkēn*)." On the other hand, Origen (*Cels.* 1.24) mentions the Stoic position that names were imposed not by convention, but by imitating the nature of things. See Verbeke, "Meaning and Role," 135.
48. For the background of this philosophical issue, see Silvermann, "Plato's *Cratylus*," 53; and Williams, "Cratylus' Theory."
49. In *Doctr. chr.* 2.16.23 (cf. 2.39.59), Augustine refers to the etymology of Hebrew names which can suggest various figurative meanings. Perhaps because Augustine's "mentor" Cicero had ridiculed the Stoic fascination with etymologies (Cicero, *Nat. d.* 3.24.61–63), Augustine initially considered the whole issue of origin of words "more a matter of curiosity than necessity" (*nimis curiosa et minus necessaria*) (*Dial.* 6). It was a matter of curiosity because it was impossible to find out the original correspondence between words and things. Nevertheless,

hermeneutics, because looking for the meaning of word-signs by employing etymological analysis helps only a little. Much more is gained by paying attention to the particular use of word-signs in their literary/syntactic context.

Non-superstitious things that humans have established are divided into "superfluous" (*superflua*) and "suitable" (*commoda*) phenomena (2.25.38). The latter, which are divided, in turn, into that which can be perceived either with "senses" (*ad sensum*) or "mind" (*ad rationem*) (2.27.41), can suggest "countless kinds of significations" (*innumerabilia genera significationum*) (2.25.39) of the conventional signs. Such conventional signs enable societies to function properly and consequently, the knowledge of these signs is necessary for understanding figurative discourse in Scripture. Augustine emphasizes particularly the benefits of knowing history and chronology (2.28.42–44), as well as topography, zoology, astronomy, logic, definitions, eloquence, numbers, and philosophy (2.29.45–2.40.61). All such things are valuable in "solving puzzles in Scripture" (*ad aenigmata scripturarum solvenda*) (2.29.45).[50] In other words, the knowledge of such things helps to understand "what Scripture wishes to convey when it includes figurative expressions" (*quid scriptura velit insinuare cum . . . figuratas locutiones inserit*) (2.30.47).

This lengthy discussion serves the interest of those interpreters who encounter figurative unknown signs (2.42.63). Yet, Augustine also cautions that excessive pursuit of "secular" wisdom—the "Egyptian treasures" (2.40.60; 2.42.63) and the "useful"

---

both in *De doctrina Christiana* and especially in his exegetical works, Augustine found the etymological digressions rather beneficial (e.g., *Enarrat. Ps.* 3.1; 7.1; 33.1.4; 41.2; 45.1; 51.4; 67.36; 80.2; 82.7; *Gen. Man.* 2.10.13).

50. Augustine indeed calls for compendia of "all the places, animals, plants, and trees, or the stones or metals, and all the other unfamiliar kinds of objects mentioned in Scripture" (*ut quoscumque terrarum locos quaeve animalia vel herbas atque arbores sive lapides vel metalla incognita speciesque quaslibet scriptura commemorat*) (*Doctr. chr.* 2.39.59) and Eucherius, among others, seems to be one who responded to this call by drafting two of his treatises (i.e., *Formulae* and Book Two of *Instructionum*).

(*utile*) erudition (2.42.63)—may side-track "young people who are keen and intelligent" (*studiosis et ingeniosis adulescentibus*) from reading and learning the Word of God (2.39.58). The moral danger is that the knowledge of "secular" wisdom may puff-up, but a proud person is prevented from understanding the things of God (2.41.62).[51] Perhaps because of this, the excursus on "secular" wisdom is beautifully framed (*inclusio*) by the issue of pride/humility (2.6.7 and 2.41.62).

Book Three

Book Three begins with a wrap-up of the hermeneutical issues considered in Book Two: an interpreter, seeking God's will in Scripture, needs to know languages, things that are used for imagery and signification, and have reliable, corrected texts in order to resolve the ambiguities of scriptural statements (3.1.1).

In Book Three, Augustine assesses "ambiguous signs" (*signa ambigua*) (3.1.1).[52] The evident problem is that words as signs have an inherent capacity to signify in more than just one way.[53] Augustine divides the ambiguous signs—just like he did with the unknown signs—according to whether they are literal (*propria*) or figurative (*translata*) (3.1.1). He begins with the literal signs, which have their own reasons for being ambiguous, and comes up with several suggestions for their disambiguation.

Augustine's first rule addresses the fact that, in his time, biblical texts did not yet have sufficient punctuation, division of words, textual layouts, verse-systems, and other such helps for facilitating reading.[54] For this reason, he urges one to check the correctness

---

51. Cf. Augustine, *Conf.* 3.5.9.
52. Atherton, *Stoics on Ambiguity*; Toom, "Augustine on Ambiguity."
53. Aristotle, *Rhet.* 1407a30–1407b6; Cicero, *Inv.* 2.40.116–121; *Or.* 2.26.110–112; Quintilian, *Inst.* 7.9.1–15; Lausberg, *Handbook*, §§222–223.
54. Blumell, "Scripture as Artifact"; Ganz, "Early Manuscripts."

of punctuation or articulation (3.2.2).[55] Intonation can turn an affirmative sentence into an interrogatory one, a pause in voicing can suggest punctuation, and the length of a pronounced syllable can change the meaning of a word (3.2.3–3.3.7). Accordingly, if there is any uncertainty about punctuation or articulation, Augustine strongly recommends the following: one has to consult the rule of faith, which is supported by the plainer passages of Scripture,[56] the authority of the church, and the immediate literary context of the word or statement (3.2.2). Giving an example, Augustine evaluates a "heretical punctuation" (*haeretica distinctio*) of John 1:1–2 and shows how the rule of faith helps to exclude an inadequate reading (3.2.3). After that he turns to the example of Phil 1:22–24 and indicates how the literary context helps to determine the correct punctuation (3.2.4). The two main means of disambiguation that Augustine brings up—(1) the rule of faith and (2) the context—are mentioned together twice (3.2.5 and 3.3.6). If these two means do not solve the issue the reader will not be wrong however the passage is articulated (3.3.6).

As Augustine comes to the last group of word-signs, to ambiguous figurative signs (3.5.9), he has to address a salient issue—how to distinguish between literal and figurative signs in the first

---

55. Augustine adds "articulation" because the problems of punctuation also apply to the problems of "reading aloud" (*pronuntiationibus*) (*Doctr. chr.* 3.3.6).

56. In *Doctr. chr.* 3.2.2, Augustine reminds the reader that he considered the rule of faith "adequately" (*satis*) in Book One (*Doctr. chr.* 1.5.5–1.21.19), where he determined what Scripture was all about and where he spoke about "the things which are objects of our faith" (*de rebus continentibus fidem*) (*Doctr. chr.* 1.40.44). *Regula fidei* is Christian preunderstanding which enables understanding. For example, in *Gen. imp.* 1.2–4, and before he exegetes Genesis, Augustine confesses his catholic faith. Likewise, in *Trin.* 1.7, Augustine affirms the *regula fidei* and only then begins to assess the scriptural data. The rule of faith does not provide a "correct" interpretation, but it certainly excludes incorrect interpretations (e.g., *Civ.* 15.26). While modern, and even more postmodern, analyses of reading strongly question the validity of approaching a text with an extra-textual criterion, Augustine would have not called *regula fidei* "extra-textual" because it was but a summary of the teachings of the unambiguous texts of Scripture.

place? How to determine which is what?[57] This topic is discussed at length within the larger context of ambiguous signs.

Augustine's first counsel says, "One must take care not to interpret a figurative expression literally" (*cavendum est ne figuratam locutionem ad litteram accipias*) (3.5.9; 3.10.14). His second counsel is a mirror-image of the first: "not to accept a literal [expression] as if it were figurative" (*ne propriam quasi figuratam velimus accipere*) (3.10.14).

In the first case, not to recognize the cases where utterances are meant to be taken figuratively, or worse still, to literalize the intended metaphorical discourse, is to read Scripture "carnally" (*carnaliter*) (3.5.9 and 3.6.11). "Carnal" reading means not understanding words in their intended referential function and being "incapable" (*non posse*) of discerning any second level signification of words (3.5.9 and 3.9.13).[58]

So, what is one supposed to do? How to avoid such interpretative errors? Augustine stipulates his famous general advice:

> Anything in the divine discourse that cannot be related either to good morals or to the true faith should be taken as figurative (*ut quidquid in sermone divino neque ad morum honestatem neque ad fidei veritatem proprie referri potest figuratum esse cognoscas*) (3.10.14)

By "good morals," Augustine means, above all, the requirement of keeping the double commandment of love.[59] Since this commandment is the *res* and the *skopos* of Scripture (Matt

---

57. Plato complained that "the young can't distinguish what is allegorical from what isn't" (*Resp.* 378d). Bernard calls this issue the "Gordian knot" of Augustine's hermeneutics (Bernard, "Unnoticed Excursus.").

58. What Augustine arguably has in mind are humans who are not able to recognize the intelligible behind the sensible, as well as Jews who are not able to recognize Christological references in the "old" dispensation (*Doctr. chr.* 3.5.9–3.7.11; cf. 2.1.1; 2.10.15; and 3.37.56).

59. Pollmann, *Doctrina Christiana*, 121–47 (see esp. the paragraph titled, "Die hermeneutische Valenz der caritas," [135–43]), where she discusses the question of why Augustine gave so much textual space to this topic in his hermeneutics. The answer is that the *caritas*-ethics is the goal hermeneutics (see also Owens, "Role of *Caritas*," 17–47; and Pool, "No Entrance").

22:40),[60] and since knowing the *res* makes referential *signa* meaningful, love is made "the *terminus* of all biblical signification."[61] "Love is the fulfillment of the law" (Rom 13:10 quoted in 1.35.39). This is the reason why Augustine settles on *caritas* as the ultimate criterion, while combining the Golden Rule (Tob 4:15; Matt 7:12) with the double commandment of love (3.10.15–3.12.20; 3.1.4.22). It follows that any interpretation which fails "to build up this double love of God and neighbor" (*non aedificet istam geminam caritatem dei et proximi*) is ultimately a misinterpretation—even if it seems to conform to the (humanly) intended meaning of a passage and happens to be "correct" in some secondary aspects (1.36.40–1.37.41).

So, Augustine postulates another wonderful general rule:

> The passage being read should be studied with careful consideration until its interpretation can be connected with the realm of love. If this point is made literally, then no kind of figurative expression needs to be considered (*ut dam diu versetur diligenti consideratione quod legitur donec ad regnum caritatis interpretatio perducatur. Si autem hoc iam proprie sonat, nulla putetur figurata locutio*) (3.13.23; cf. 1.36.40; 1.40.44).[62]

Such a rule has an enormous hermeneutical significance, for only keeping the criterion *caritas* (or the *res* of Scripture) always in front of his/her (mental) eyes, an exegete can interpret the *signa* properly and determine whether these have to be taken figuratively or literally.

However, Augustine is not naïve about his recommended rules. He is fully aware of the fact that "good morals" and "love" can prove to be rather ambiguous criteria due to people's varied cultural, societal, as well as individual ethical convictions (3.10.15; 3.14.22). Accordingly, a decision to take something literally or

---

60. Augustine, *Catech.* 4.8; 26.50; *Doctr. chr.* 1.22.21; 1.26.27–1.30.33; 1.35.39–1.36.41; 3.12.20; *Enarrat. Ps.* 103.1.9; 140.2.
61. Babcock, "*Caritas* and Signification," 154.
62. In the list of moral prerequisites for interpreting Scripture, the third step that Augustine mentions is knowledge (*scientia*). It concerns the full awareness of the fact that Scripture teaches the double commandment of love (*Doctr. chr.* 2.7.10).

figuratively can often be dependent merely on people's subjective preferences and perceptions of "good morals" and "love" (3.10.15). Nevertheless, being a moral realist, Augustine is quite convinced that the diversity of customs and convictions cannot relativize the notions of good and bad altogether (3.14.22). Despite the varied customs and convictions, everyone is capable of knowing what is good and loving, and what is not. This is the reason why it is not possible to completely annul and dismiss the hermeneutical criteria of "good morals" and "love."

The examples that follow concern the prescriptive sayings in Scripture and illustrate the danger of accepting literal expressions as if these were figurative (i.e., the second case). If an expression forbids wickedness and cruelty, it should be taken literally indeed (3.16.24). And vice versa, if taken literally, and it seems to recommend wickedness or cruelty, it should be taken figuratively. Also, if someone is, "or thinks he is" (*vel esse se putat*), on a higher spiritual level, various instructions for those who are not on the same level may seem figurative (3.17.25). And indeed, Augustine formulates yet another sub-rule here:

> We must understand that that some instructions are given to all people alike, but others to particular classes of people (*ut sciamus alia omnibus communiter praecipi, alias singulis quibusque generibus personarum*) (3.17.27).[63]

A special dilemma is whether to take the accounts of the immoral deeds of the Old Testament patriarchs literally or figuratively. Augustine first attempts to excuse the patriarchs' behavior with different times, circumstances, and duties (3.18.26–3.21.31).[64] These cases should be interpreted figuratively when the particular examples do not fit with the "good morals," as this is understood after the coming of the Lord. Or, better still, the warning of these cases against pride should be taken literally, despite the fact that such misdeeds may also provide a "trace of prefiguration of future

---

63. This relates to Tyconius's rules number four and five (synechdoche) which are discussed in Augustine, *Doctr. chr.* 3.34.47–3.35.51.

64. Cf. Augustine, *Gen. litt.* 9.8.13–9.10.18.

events in them" (*in eis figuram rerum futurarum . . . potuerit*) (3.23.33).

Taking the historical events or their descriptions figuratively rests on Augustine's understanding of history and prophecy.[65] He urges that narratives in Scripture should not be taken "only historically and literally but also figuratively and prophetically" (*non solum historice ac proprie sed etiam figurate ac prophetice*) (3.12.20; cf. 3.22.32).[66] For Augustine, history and prophecy are a kind of double feature of the scriptural discourse.[67] Accordingly, narratives and utterances of the past should always be read "prophetically"; that is, so that they also indicate something about the redemption history in Christ.[68] For example, quoting Ezek 36:23–29, Augustine concludes, "That is a prophecy about the New Testament" (*Hoc de novo testamento esse prophetatum*), and quoting Ezek 38:26, he links the promise with Christ (3.34.48).[69]

In *Doctr. chr.* 3.24.34, and after about thirteen pages of discussion, Augustine repeats his exhortation, "The greatest care must therefore be taken to determine whether the expression that we are trying to understand is literal or figurative" (*Maxime itaque investigandum est utrum propria sit an figurata locutio quam intellegere conamur*). And at least for a while, Augustine seems

65. Augustine, *Civ.* 15.27; 16.2; 17.1; 18.38–39; *Gen. Man.* 2.2.3; 2.24.37.
66. Cf. Augustine, *Civ.* 15.27; 16.2. Augustine compares history and prophecy to water and wine in the miracle Jesus performed in Cana. To consider history alone is "water," but to recognize Christ to whom history points (i.e., prophecy) is "wine" (*Tract. Ev. Jo.* 9.3–5, 10).
67. Markus, *Saeculum*, 187–96 (cf. Adrian, *Isag.* 74; Junillus, *Inst.* 1.3–4).
68. 1 Cor 10:11; Col 2:16–17; Augustine, *Enarrat. Ps.* 143.1; *Civ.* 18.38–39; *Tract. Ev. Jo.* 28.9 (together with New Testament prooftexts); Bochet, *Le firmament*, 477–98; Fiedrowicz contends that, for this basic conviction, Augustine took the lead from Ps 102:18 ("Let this be recorded for a generation to come") (Fiedrowicz, "General Introduction," 23).
69. The very first thing that Augustine says in his mammoth commentary on the psalms is that the first line of the first psalm refers to Lord Jesus Christ (*Enarrat. Ps.* 1.1). In *Enarrat. Ps.* 21.2.15, Augustine explains that in Christ the Scripture, which was sealed by wax, started melting. In *Enarrat. Ps.* 73.2, he further contends that there is little in the gospels that is not found in prophets already.

to be confident that the rules he has provided so far offer sufficient help for distinguishing between literal and figurative statements.

However, and next to other plausible reasons, precisely this very issue may have caused a "writer's block" for Augustine, because here (3.25.36) the original composition of *De doctrina Christiana* comes to a long halt.[70] Were these rules he had provided so far really sufficient for distinguishing between literal and figurative statements? It seems significant that as soon as Augustine begins to address the issue of figurative use of words once more, he realizes that there is really no "hard and fast rule" (*praescriptum*) about how words signify figuratively (3.25.35).

While smoothly continuing the composition of his treatise after a thirty-year break in 426 (or 427) and pondering (arguably) over the issue of how to distinguish more adequately between literal and figurative word-signs for a long time, Augustine first picks up the topic of ambiguity which comes from figurative usage of words.[71] Figurative use of words can be based on the similarity between things, on their connectedness (3.25.34), or on things being either contrary or diverse (3.25.36).[72] Consequently, the same scriptural word may have "two or more meanings" (*duo vel plura sentiuntur*) (3.27.38; cf. 3.2.2 [*pluribus*]), depending on a particular context (3.25.37).[73] This is significant, especially in the light of the modern conviction that texts, when approached "scientifi-

---

70. Augustine, *Retract.* 2.4.1. The oldest manuscript of Augustine's works, St. Petersburg manuscript Q.v.I.3, contains only the incomplete *De doctrina Christiana*.

71. It is not entirely clear what the Latin word *quod* in *Doctr. chr.* 3.25.34 refers to, but presumably Augustine has figurative statements in mind, because the whole section (3.5.9–3.29.41) is about ambiguous figurative signs.

72. Here the dependence of Eucherius's *Formulae* on Augustine is particularly manifest (see the footnotes indicating Eucherius' sources in Eucherius, *Œuvres exégétiques*, 91–259). Both authors, Augustine and Eucherius, were evidently, and in turn, aided by the discussion of Tyconius who assessed the contrary meanings of words in his *Liber regularum*.

73. Cf. Augustine, *Conf.* 12.30.41–12.32.43.

cally," have just one "right" meaning.⁷⁴ Augustine calls the phenomenon of the multiplicity of meanings an "abundant" (*largius*) and "generous" (*uberius*) gift (3.27.38).⁷⁵ It does not mean, however, that text can mean whatever. And here, Augustine appeals again to authorial intention (*voluntas*) as to a decisive criterion for determining the meaning of an utterance (3.27.38; cf. 1.36.41).⁷⁶ He has already explained that usually context is a pointer to "the writer's intention" (*scriptorum intentio*) (3.4.8). Yet, even if the authorial intention remains undiscoverable or is obscure,⁷⁷ other passages in Scripture help to decide whether a particular interpretation "is consistent with the truth" (*congruere veritati*) (3.27.38).⁷⁸ And to do so, Augustine guardedly recommends using one's reason (*ratio*) (3.28.39).⁷⁹

In the case of Scripture, however and as it was mentioned earlier, it is not sufficient to take into consideration the human authorial intention only, because God is believed to be the ultimate *author* of Scripture. Therefore, Augustine explains yet again that he means "the intention of the writer through whom the Holy Spirit produced that part of Scripture" (*ut ad voluntatem perveniantur*

---

74. Briggs, "Premodern Interpretation"; Toom, "Augustine's Case." In fact, and perhaps surprisingly, even Schleiermacher wrote, "One cannot discuss allegorical interpretation with the general principle that every utterance could only have one meaning" (Schleiermacher, *Hermeneutics and Criticism*, 15).

75. See Bochet, "règles pour l'interprétation," 46–48; Bochet and Madec, "Pluralité des interprétations." In *Gen. imp.* 2.5 and *Util. cred.* 3.5–9, Augustine states his own version of the *quadriga* (cf. Cassian, *Conl.* 11 [Preface] and 14.8; and Eucherius, *Form.* Praef. 52–53, 56–58), but after 390s, he never mentions it again. It is plausible that as he was composing *De doctrina Christiana*, he came up with a more profound system of word-signs which included all possible cases.

76. Cf. Augustine, *Cons.* 2.46.97.

77. The difficulty of appealing to and operating with authorial intention is discussed in Augustine, *Civ.* 11.19, 33; *Conf.* 12.18.27; 23.32–24.33; *Tract. Ev. Jo.* 1.1.

78. This advice is most helpfully summarized in *Gen. litt.* 1.21.41, where Augustine teaches that, in the case of several legitimate interpretations, on has to prefer those which (1) the author intended; (2) the context supports; and (3) the sound faith/truth affirms.

79. Cf. Augustine, *Gen. litt.* 10.16.29; 10.23.29.

auctoris per quem scripturam illam sanctus operatus est spiritus) (3.27.38; cf. 2.5.6).[80] The human writers of Scripture may or may not have fully understood the Spirit's intention, but God certainly has managed to say what God wanted to say to the readers of Scripture in any time. To put this differently, due to the multiplicity of meanings, God can say more than (the inspired) humans intend to say and/or manage to say in writing Scripture.[81] Does not Apostle Paul say, "What I am saying . . . I do not say the way the Lord would" (2 Cor 11:1; cf. 1 Cor 7:10, 12, 25, 40)?

Augustine takes a look at yet another cause of ambiguity which is Scripture's use of figures of speech or tropes,[82] adding immediately that his treatise is not about teaching grammar and figures of speech (3.29.40).[83] He thinks that such things should be learned separately, just like any other kind of "secular" education is supposed to be acquired separately (cf. 2.17.27–2.42.63; cf. 4.1.2). Nevertheless, Augustine mentions several tropes, as if not being able to resist the urge to hint at his thorough knowledge of such things (3.29.40–41).

While insisting on the fact that one's knowledge of figures of speech helps indeed to disambiguate texts, Augustine also states something fundamental for hermeneutics. In addition to the rules about distinguishing between literal and figurative signs in Book Three before the interruption, he now worded yet another general rule, a third one:

> When a meaning based on the literal interpretation of the words is absurd (*quia cum sensus, ad proprietatem verborum se accipiatur, absur-*

---

80. Smith, "Complex Authorial Intention"; Toom, "Was Augustine an Intentionalist?"

81. "Since he [the evangelist John] was a human being, even though inspired, he did not say everything, but he said only what he could say as a human being" (*quia uero homo inspiratus, non totum quod est dixit, sed quod potuit homo, dixit*) (Augustine, *Tract. Ev. Jo.* 1.1).

82. Lausberg, *Handbook*, §§522–599. See Cameron, "Figures of Speech"; Wagner, "Rhetorical Distinctions."

83. Unlike Augustine, the author of another *introductio*, Adrian, takes the trouble to address the issue of tropes in his treatise about Scripture and its interpretation (*Isag.* 73.1–22).

dus est), one must investigate whether the difficult passage is using tropes and whether it has to be interpreted figuratively (3.29.41).[84]

Augustine probably knew about the so-called "absurdity criterion" since the days of his studies,[85] and stated it first in his *De Genesi contra Manichaeos* (389 CE).[86] It contends that if a literal statement is absurd, one has to seek the meaning of a text on another level, on a figurative level.[87] Or, put differently, if that which the text says literally is blasphemous and unworthy of God, it has to be taken in another way.[88] For example, harsh and cruel words attributed to God and saints in Scripture should be taken figuratively, because these contradict what God and saint are taken to be (3.11.17–3.12.18). In *Doctr. chr.* 3.3.6, Augustine considers a particular interpretation "crazy" (*dementissimum*) and suggests that another meaning of the statement should be sought. Even in his literal commentary on Genesis, Augustine often has no option but to consider figurative interpretation(s), because there is no evident meaning to what the text says *kata lexin*.[89] This means that if something in Scripture seems problematic, it should be taken as

---

84. Cf. Augustine, *Enarrat. Ps.* 45.9; 59.2; *Gen. litt.* 5.8.23; 8.2.5; 9.12.22; 11.1.2; Ambrose, *Fug.* 2.13; Cassian, *Inst.* 8.3; Hilary, *Comm. in Matt.* 25.2; Origen, *PArch.* 4.3.1–5; Philo, *Queast. in Gen.* 1.45; and Tyconius, *Reg.* 1.10.105.

85. Pépin, "A propos de l'histoire."

86. Augustine, *Gen. Man.* 1.22.34; 2.2.3; Evans, "*Absurditas*"; Teske, "Criteria."

87. "Generally, it is only when a sentence is taken to be false that we accept it as a metaphor and start to hunt out the hidden implication" (Davidson, "What Metaphors Mean," 40). However, the absurdity of purely literal reading of text is not the only reason for figurative interpretation. The main reason for figurative interpretation is that texts can point beyond their "original" meaning, and thus they have to be related to the overall salvation history and read in the light of the Christ-event.

88. Cf. Augustine, *Enarrat. Ps.* 68.1.10; 82.12;130.12; *Gen. Man.* 2.2.3; *Gen. litt.* 5.19.39.

89. For example, Augustine rejects an absurd interpretation of Gen 2:2 (God rested on the seventh day) by saying that one could not possibly imagine that God was exhausted (*Gen. litt.* 4.28.45). Thus, the text has to mean something else.

referring to something figuratively "because plain silly it cannot be" (*quia stultum esse non potest*).[90]

Yet Augustine provides a caveat even for this mighty "absurdity criterion": "This is how *most* hidden meanings have been discovered" (*Et sic pleraque inventa sunt quae latebant*)" (3.29.41 [emphasis mine]). It evidently means that none of the criteria for distinguishing between literal and figurative statements proves to be absolute and infallible. Even the absurdity criterion is inevitably dependent on human convictions and preferences.[91] At the end of the day, making a distinction between literal and figurative statements is an interpretative art rather than a technique which slavishly follows instructions.[92]

In the larger context of ambiguous figurative signs, right after stating the "absurdity criterion" and while considering tropes, Augustine also introduces Tyconius's *Liber regularum*, assesses it critically, and recommends it cautiously. The placement of Tyconius's rules is significant. After realizing that, in fact, there are really no rules which would infallibly distinguish between literal and figurative statements, Augustine takes on Tyconius's promise that knowing his rules would open whatever (*quaeque*) was closed and illumine whatever was obscure in Scripture (Tyconius, *Reg.* Praef. 7).[93] Augustine is not so optimistic at all (*Doctr. chr.* 3.30.42–43). Nevertheless, he considers Tyconius's

---

90. Augustine, *Gen. litt.* 9.12.22 (repeated in 9.13.23).

91. In *Conf.* 6.4.6, Augustine admits that what he considered absurd as a Manichee, he no longer considered absurd as a Christian. Philo of Alexandria, for example, considered the prohibition in Exod 12:9a "Do not eat raw meat!" absurd, because no one in their right mind would eat raw meat. It has to be taken allegorically (*Quaest. Exo.* 1.16). But people actually do eat raw meat (steak *tartare*!), and this prohibition is not equally absurd for everyone in every place and in every time.

92. What Davidson says about metaphors is true about figurative utterances generally, "There is no manual for determining what a metaphor 'means' or 'says'; there is no test for metaphor that does not call for taste" ("What Metaphors Mean," 29). For the concept of "guidance," as distinguished from mechanistic rule-following, see Smith, *Scriptures*, 22–32.

93. Vercruysse, *Tyconius: Le Livre des Règles*, 130; Babcock, *Tyconius*, 3.

proposals to be "quite helpful" (*non parvum adiuvant*) and even "very helpful" (*plurimum adiuvat*) (3.30.32–34), as these aid in determining the changing referents in Scripture.[94]

In addition to his main topic (i.e., the changes of references), Tyconius considers the figures of speech—both of which create ambiguity—and employs the absurdity criterion (without explicitly naming it so).[95] All this fits with Augustine's discussion of hermeneutics in Book Three. Immediately before bringing in Tyconius's rules, Augustine recalls his main topic of discussion (i.e., ambiguous figurative signs[96]) once again and states that recognizing the literary tropes and the plurality of possible referents "is necessary for the resolution of ambiguities in scripture" (*Quorum cognitio propterea scripturarum ambiguitatibus dissolvendis est necessaria*) (3.29.41). These are Tyconius's contentions in his *Liber regularum* as well.

Finally, and once again, interpreting Scripture requires the right disposition and divine illumination. Augustine cites Prov 2:6, "God gives wisdom, and from his face there is knowledge and understanding" (3.37.56) and reminds his readers that they need to pray. "This is paramount, and absolutely vital—to pray for understanding" (*quod est praecipuum et maxime necessarium, orent ut intellegant*) (3.37.56).[97] After all, Luke 24:45 says, "Then he opened their minds so they could understand the Scriptures." In Book One, Augustine identified knowledge (*scientia*) as the third stage of the "ladder" of spiritual progress and added that knowledge was gained by praying for divine assistance. Thus, the topic

---

94. Toom, "Tyconius' *Liber regularum*."
95. In *Reg.* 1.10.105, Tyconius says explicitly, "Nor is it absurd . . ." (*Nec illud erit absurdum . . .*).
96. Augustine points out that what is characteristic to figurative speech (*tropicae locutionis*) is that "one thing is said in order that something else may be understood" (*ubicumque velut aliud dicitur ut aliud intellegatur*) (*Doctr. chr.* 3.37.56; cf. *Enarrat. Ps.* 103.1.13). Variants of this definition are also cited by other *introductores* listed in Cassiodorus, *Inst.* 1.10, such as Junillus, *Inst.* 1.5 and Adrian, *Isag.* 73.13. For classical examples, see Lausberg, *Handbook*, §§895–901.
97. A similar point is made by Augustine, *Doctr. chr.* Praef. 8; Cassian, *Inst.* 5.33–34; *Conl.* 14.9; Cassiodorus, *Inst.* 1, Praef. 7; 1.28.2, 32.6.

of prayer is a kind of *inclusio* for the hermeneutical advice in Books Two and Three of *De doctrina Christiana* (2.7.10; 3.37.56). And the purpose of an *inclusio* is to highlight a particularly important theme.

Conclusion

This article has highlighted the main hermeneutical topics and the corresponding interpretative advice that Augustine has decided to discuss in Books Two and Three of his *De doctrina Christiana*. As can be seen from the many footnotes, these topics are also stated and explicated upon in the other works of Augustine.

Augustine begins his consideration of hermeneutics by saying a few things about the right disposition of a would-be interpreter of Scripture, about one's moral and spiritual condition, as well as one's attitude towards his hermeneutical advice (*Prol.*). And he ends Book Three by emphasizing the necessity of prayer. This means that, according to Augustine, understanding Scripture cannot be reduced to a mere intellectual effort unaided by divine grace and illumination.[98] *Scientia* has to come after *timor* and *pietas* (2.7.10).

Within this larger framework of his treatise, Augustine is focusing on intentional word-signs (*signa data*), which express both the human and the divine intentions in Scripture and which have been translated into various languages. Consequently, an interpreter has to learn languages in order to compare the Latin versions of Scripture with those in Greek and Hebrew and establish the best text possible. Also, an interpreter has to determine the proper hermeneutical object which is the canonical Scripture. A general principle for interpreting the canonical Scripture is that plainer passages explain the more obscure passages, as everything is believed to cohere in the Word of God. Another piece of advice is to pay attention to the immediate literary context of an utterance, to follow the *regula fidei*, and to apprehend, in the deep

---

98. Augustine begins his commentary on the Gospel of John by citing 1 Cor 2:14, "The person without the Spirit does not accept the things that come from the Spirit of God" (*Tract. Ev. Jo.* 1.1).

sense of this word, that Scripture teaches *caritas*. Having a good "secular" education facilitates, in turn, one's comprehension of the analogies and the figures of speech that Scripture employs. Affirming the multiplicity of meanings, Augustine tackles the problem of how to distinguish between literal and figurative expressions. He suggests three rules of thumb: (1) what is contrary to good morals and the true faith has to be taken figuratively; (2) what does not promote *caritas* has to be taken figuratively; and (3) what is absurd, has to be taken figuratively. These are, pretty much the hermeneutical topics that Augustine considers while discussing signification in Books Two and Three of his *De doctrina Christiana*.

Bibliography

Andrews, James A. *Hermeneutics and the Church: In Dialogue with Augustine*. Notre Dame: Notre Dame University Press, 2012.

Atherton, Catherine. *The Stoics on Ambiguity*. Cambridge: Cambridge University Press, 1993.

Augustine. *De Doctrina Christiana*, edited and translated by R. P. H. Green. Oxford Early Christian Texts. Oxford: Clarendon, 1995.

Babcock, William S. "*Caritas* and Signification in *De doctrina christiana* 1–3." In *De doctrina christiana: A Classic of Western Culture*, edited by Duane W. H. Arnold and Pamela Bright, 145–63. Christianity and Judaism in Antiquity 9. Notre Dame: University of Notre Dame Press, 1995.

———. *Tyconius: The Book of Rules*. Society of Biblical Literature: Texts and Translations 31. Atlanta: Scholars, 1989.

Bernard, Robert W. "An Unnoticed Excursus in Augustine of Hippo's *De doctrina Christiana*: A Gordian Knot on his

Exegetical Theory." *American Society of Church History Meeting* (1997) 1–25. Microfiche.

Blumell, Lincoln H. "Scripture as Artifact." In *The Oxford Handbook of Early Christian Biblical Interpretation*, edited by Paul M. Blowers and Peter Martens, 7–32. Oxford: Oxford University Press, 2019.

Bochet, Isabelle. *Le firmament de l'Écriture: L'heméneutique augustinienne*. Série antiquité 172. Paris: Insititut d'études augustiniennes, 2004.

———. "Les règles pour l'interprétation de l'Écriture: le *De doctrina christiana* d'Augustin." *Connaissance des Pères de l'Église* 131 (2013) 41–51.

Bochet, Isabelle, and Goulven Madec. "Le canon des Écritures, la Septante et d'Itala." In *La doctrine chrétienne: De doctrina chrisitana*. Œuvres de saint Augustin 11.2, 506–23. Paris: Institut d'études augustiniennes, 1997.

———. "Pluralité des interpretations scripturaires." In *La doctrine chrétienne: De doctrina chrisitana*. Œuvres de saint Augustin 11.2, 558–62. Paris: Institut d'études augustiniennes, 1997.

———. "Les signes." In *La doctrine chrétienne: De doctrina chrisitana*. Œuvres de saint Augustin 11.2, 483–95. Paris: Institut d'études augustiniennes, 1997.

Bogaert, Pierre Maurice. "Les livres d'Esdras et leur numérotation dans l'histoire du canon de la Bible latine." *Revue bénédictine* 110 (2000) 5–26.

———. "Les bibles d'Augustin." *Revue théologique de Louvain* 37 (2006) 513–31.

Bonnardière, Anne-Marie la. "Le canon des divines Écritures." In Anne-Marie la Bonnardière, *Saint Augustin et la Bible*, 287–310. Bible de tous les temps 3. Paris: Beauchesne, 1986.

Borsche, Tilman. "Zeichentheorie im Übergang von den Stoikern zu Augustin." *Allgemeine Zeitschrift für Pilosophie* 19 (1994) 41–52.

Briggs, Richard S. "Premodern Interpretation and Contemporary Exegesis." In *The New Cambridge Companion to Biblical Interpretation*, edited by Ian Boxall and Bradley C. Gregory, 301–17. Cambridge: Cambridge University Press, 2023.

Cameron, Michael. *Christ Meets Me Everywhere: Augustine's Early Figurative Exegesis*. Oxford Studies in Historical Theology. Oxford: Oxford University Press, 2012.

———. "Figures of Speech and Knowledge of God in Augustine's Early Biblical Interpretation." *Augustinian Studies* 38 (2007) 61–85.

Cary, Phillip. *Outward Signs: The Powerlessness of External Things in Augustine's Thought*. Oxford: Oxford University Press, 2008.

Davidson, Donald. "What Metaphors Mean." In *On Metaphor*, edited by Sheldon Sacks, 29–45. Chicago: University of Chicago Press, 1979.

Eucherius, *Œuvres exégétiques: Clés pour l'intelligence spirituelle; Instructions*, edited and translated by Carmela Mandolfo and Martine Dulaey. Sources chrétiennes 618. Paris: Éditions du Cerf, 2021.

Evans, Gillian R. "*Absurditas* in Augustine's Scriptural Commentary." *Downside Review* 99 (1981) 109–18.

Fiedrowicz, Michael. "General Introduction." Translated by Maria Boulding. In *Expositions of the Psalms*, edited by John E. Rotelle, 13–66. The Works of Saint Augustine: A Translation for the 21st Century 3/15. New York: New City, 2000.

Gallagher, Edmon L., and John D. Meade. *The Biblical Canon Lists from Early Christianity: Texts and Analysis*. Oxford: Oxford University Press, 2017.

Ganz, David. "Early Manuscripts of the Latin Bible." In *The Oxford Handbook of the Latin Bible*, edited by Hugh A. G. Houghton, 106–20. Oxford: Oxford University Press, 2023.

Gramigna, Remo. *Augustine's Theory of Signs, Signification, and Lying*. Semiotics in Religion 3. Berlin: de Gruyter, 2020.

Houghton, Hugh A. G. "The Earliest Latin Translations of the Bible." In *The Oxford Handbook of the Latin Bible*, edited by Hugh A. G. Houghton, 1–18. Oxford: Oxford University Press, 2023.

Istace, G. "Le livre Ier du *De doctrina christiana* de saint Augustin." *Ephemerides Theologicae Lovanienses* 32 (1956) 289–330.

Jackson, Belford Darrel. *Augustine: De dialectica*. Synthese Historical Library 16. Dordrecht: D. Reidel, 1975.

———. "Semantics and Hermeneutics in Saint Augustine's *De doctrina Christiana*." PhD diss., Yale University, 1967.

James, Mark R. *Learning the Language of Scripture: Origen, Wisdom, and the Logic of Interpretation*. Studies in Systematic Theology 24. Leiden: Brill, 2021.

Kamimura, Naoki. "Augustine's Scriptural Exegesis in *De sermon Domini in monte* and the Shaping of Christian

Perfection." In *Christians Shaping Identity from the Roman Empire to Byzantium*, edited by Geoffrey Dunn and Wendy Mayer, 225–47. Vigiliae Christianae Supplements 132. Leiden: Brill, 2015.

King, Peter. "Augustine on Language." In *The Cambridge Companion to Augustine*, edited by David V. Meconi and Eleanore Stump, 292–310. 2nd ed. Cambridge: Cambridge University Press, 2014.

Lange, Armin. "The History of the Christian Old Testament Canon." In *The Hebrew Bible: Overview Articles*, edited by Armin Lange and Emanuel Tov, 48a-81b. Textual History of the Bible 1A. Leiden: Brill, 2016.

Lausberg, Heinrich. *Handbook of Literary Rhetoric*. Translated by Matthew T. Bliss et al. Leiden: Brill, 1998.

Lierde, Peter Canisius Johannes van. "The Teaching of St. Augustine on the Gifts of the Holy Spirit from the Text of Isaiah 11:2–3." Translated by Joseph C. Schnaubelt and Frederick Van Fleteren. In *Augustine: Mystic and Mystagogue*, edited by Frederick Van Fleteren et al., 5–110. Collectanea Augustiana. New York: Peter Lang, 1994.

Manetti, Giovanni. *Theories of the Sign in Classical Antiquity*. Translated by Christine Richardson. Bloomington: Indiana University Press, 1993.

Markus, Robert A. *Saeculum: History and Society in the Theology of St. Augustine*. Cambridge: Cambridge University Press, 1970.

———. *Signs and Meanings: World and Text in Ancient Christianity*. Liverpool: Liverpool University Press, 1996.

———. "St. Augustine on Signs." *Phronesis* 2 (1957) 60–83.

Munier, Charles. "La tradition manuscrite de l'Abrégé d'Hippone et le canon des Écritures des églises africaines." *Sacris Erudiri* 21 (1972–1973) 43–55.

O'Loughlin, Thomas. "The Structure of the Collections that Make Up the Scriptures: The Influence of Augustine on Cassiodorus." *Revue bénédictine* 124 (2014) 48–64.

Owens, Briant K. "The Role of *Caritas* in the Hermeneutics of Saint Augustine and Its Impact on Philosophical and Theological Hermeneutics." PhD diss., Faulkner University, 2018.

Pépin, Jean. "À propos de l'histoire de l'exégèse allégorique: l'absurdité, signe de l'allégorie." *Studia Patristica* 1 (1957) 395–413.

Pollmann, Karla. *Doctrina Christiana: Untersuchungen zu den Anfängen der christlichen Heumeneutik unter besonderer Berücksichtigung von Augustinus, "De doctrina christiana."* Paradosis: Beträge zur Geschichte der altchristlichen Literatur und Theologie 41. Freiburg: Universitätsverlag, 1996.

———. "Re-Appropriation and Disavowal: Pagan and Christian Authorities in Cassiodorus and Venantius Fortunatus." In *Religious Identity and the Problem of Historical Foundation*, edited by Judith Frishman et al., 289–316. Jewish and Christian Perspectives Series 8. Leiden: Brill, 2004.

Pool, Jeff B. "No Entrance into Truth Except through Love: Contributions from Augustine of Hippo to a Contemporary Christian Hermeneutics of Love." *Review & Expositor* 101 (2004) 629–66.

Reíllo, José M. C. "The Latin Bible and the Septuagint." In *The Oxford Handbook of the Latin Bible*, edited by Hugh A. G. Houghton, 19–36. Oxford: Oxford University Press, 2023.

Schildenberger, Johannes. "Die Itala des heiligen Augustinus." In *Colligere Fragmenta: Festschrift Alban Dold zum 70. Geburtstag am 7. 7. 1952*, edited by Bonifatius Fischer et al., 84–102. Texte und Arbeiten 1. Beuron: Kunstverlag, 1952.

Schirner, Rebekka S. *Inspice diligenter codices: Philosogische Studien zu Augustins Umgang mit Bibelhandschriften und übersetzungen*. Millennium-Studien 49. Berlin: de Gruyter, 2015.

Schleiermacher, Friedrich. *Hermeneutics and Criticism: And Other Writings*. Translated and edited by Andrew Bowie. Cambridge Texts in the History of Philosophy. Cambridge: Cambridge University Press, 1998.

Schultheiß, Jochen. "Augustinus, *De doctrina Christiana*." In *Handbuch der Bibelhermeneutiken: von Origenes bis zur Gengenwart*, edited by Oda Wischmeyer et al., 47–61. Berlin: de Gruyter, 2016.

Schulz-Flügel, Eva. "Der lateinische Bibeltext im 4. Jahrhundert." In *Augustin Handbuch*, edited by Volker H. Drecoll, 109–14. Tübingen: Mohr Siebeck, 2007.

Sieben, Hermann-Josef. "Die 'res' der Bibel: Eine Analyse von Augustinus, *De doctr. Christ.* I–III." *Revue d'études augustiniennes et patristiques* 21 (1975) 72–90.

Silvermann, Allan. "Plato's *Cratylus*: The Naming of Nature and the Nature of Naming." *Oxford Studies in Ancient Philosophy* 10 (1992) 25–71.

Smith, Brett W. "Complex Authorial Intention in Augustine's Hermeneutics." *Augustinian Studies* 45 (2014) 203–25.

Smith, Stephen G. *Scriptures and the Guidance of Language: Evaluating Religious Authority in Communicative Action.* Cambridge: Cambridge University Press, 2018.

Teske, Roland J. "Criteria for Figurative Interpretation in St. Augustine." In *De doctrina christiana: A Classic of Western Culture*, edited by Duane W. H. Arnold and Pamela Bright, 109–22. Christianity and Judaism in Antiquity 9. Notre Dame: University of Notre Dame Press, 1995.

Toom, Tarmo. "Ancient Christian Textbooks (*Introductiones*) on Hermeneutics." *Studia Patristica*. Forthcoming.

———. "Augustine on Ambiguity." *Augustinian Studies* 38 (2008) 407–33.

———. "Augustine's Case for the Multiplicity of Meanings." *Augustinian Studies* 45 (2014) 183–201.

———. "Augustine's Hermeneutics: The Science of the Divinely Given Signs." In *Patristic Theories of Biblical Interpretation: The Latin Fathers*, edited by Tarmo Toom, 77–108. Cambridge: Cambridge University Press, 2016.

———. "Babel, Translations, and Polysemy in Augustine's ciu. Dei XV–XVIII." *Augustinus—Werk und Wirkkung* 19 (2024). Forthcoming.

———. "Tyconius' *Liber regularum* as a Hermaneutical Treatise." *Augustinian Studies* 55 (2024) 83–105.

———. "Was Augustine an Intentionalist? Authorial Intention in Augustine's Hermeneutics." *Studia Patristica* 70 (2013) 185–93.

Verbeke, G. "Meaning and Role of the Expressible (*lekton*) in Stoic Language." In *Knowledge through Signs: Ancient Semiotic Theories and Practices*, edited by Giovanni

Manetti, Semiotic and Cognitive Studies, 133–54. Bologna: Brepols, 1996.

Vercruysse, Jean-Marc. *Tyconius: Le Livre des Règles*. Sources Chrétiennes 488. Paris: Du Cerf, 2004.

Wagner, Nathan. "Rhetorical Distinctions in Augustine's Early and Later Writing." *Rhetorica* 36 (2018) 105–31.

Williams, Bernard. "Cratylus' Theory of Names and its Refutation." In *Language*, edited by Stephen Everson, 28–36. Companions to Ancient Thought 3. Cambridge: Cambridge University Press, 1994.

Wittgenstein, Ludwig. *Philosophical Investigations*. Translated by G. E. M. Anscombe. 3rd edition. Engelwood Cliffs, NJ: Prentice Hall, 1958.

St. Augustine's Number Pneumatology

Seung Heon (Hosea) Sheen
Regent College, Vancouver, BC, Canada

Introduction and Context

In studying the theological career of St. Augustine of Hippo (354–430 AD), scholars have often employed a framework that pits the early optimist Christian philosopher Augustine against the later pessimist bishop Augustine. Peter Brown's famous depiction of the "lost future" is exemplary for such opinions on Augustine's theological career.[1] Although the once popular claim that Augustine went through "two conversions"—first to Neoplatonism in 386 and eventually to Christianity in 396—has lost support in Augustine scholarship, the more subtle depiction of the "two Augustines" is still very much popular.[2] However, this framework of discontinuity has been challenged by scholars such as Carol Harrison, who argues that there is in fact a significant continuity between his early and later works.[3] These advocates of "continuity" argue that even in his earlier more philosophical works, Augustine's Neoplatonism was always mediated and regulated by his understanding of the Christian tradition, which did not change dramatically in his more mature works.[4] But this is not to disregard the possibility of a gradual intellectual development in Augustine, due to a maturing reflection on the Christian Scriptures

---

1. Brown, *Augustine of Hippo*, 139–50.
2. Harrison, *Rethinking Augustine's Early Theology*, 15–19.
3. Harrison, *Rethinking Augustine's Early Theology*.
4. For example, Harrison identifies the themes of human dependence and the primacy of grace in Augustine's early works (*Rethinking Augustine's Early Theology*, 72–73). Similarly, Michel Barnes and Lewis Ayres have made similar arguments regarding Augustine's trinitarian theology (see Barnes, "De Regnon Reconsidered"; Ayres, *Augustine and the Trinity*).

and doctrines, as well as a corresponding philosophical reevaluation. Notably for this paper, Chad Gerber has traced the development of Augustine's pro-Nicene pneumatology in his early works, in which the Spirit's role as Love and sustainer of form becomes increasingly clarified.[5] *De libero arbitrio* (*Lib.*) is a particularly interesting work with regards to this debate, since it was written over the long period between 387 and 395: *laicus coepi, presbyter explicavi* ("began as a layman, finished as a presbyter").[6] In a sense, the work as a whole reveals the thought of both the early and more mature Augustine, and thus it is an important text for understanding his intellectual development.[7] As one would expect in such a work, elements characteristic of both his early philosophical writings and latter more explicitly doctrinal writings are identifiable in it. Particularly for our purposes, *Lib.* 2, composed in Hippo after his ordination in 391, serves as a useful text for attempting to understand the early theology—both philosophical and doctrinal—of Augustine the priest.[8]

An often-neglected aspect of Augustine's early philosophical formation is his reception of Neopythagoreanism. In the Neopythagorean tradition—a strand of Middle Platonism and Neoplatonism which emphasized the mathematical sciences (especially arithmetic and music)—*number* (ἀριθμός, *numerus*) names the fundamental principle of rationality and harmony that undergirds the coherent existence of the cosmos and all individual beings within it.[9] For example, for Nicomachus of Gerasa, num-

---

5. Gerber, *Spirit of Augustine's Early Theology.*
6. Augustine, *Persev.* 12.30.
7. See, e.g., Harrison, *Augustine's Way into the Will,* 17–27.
8. Saint Augustine of Hippo, *On the Free Choice of the Will,* xvii.
9. In fact, Neopythagoreanism likely had very little to do with the historical Pythagoras and his followers, for it was more so an intellectual movement of mathematicising Platonism rather than a continuation of the pre-Socratic philosophical school which Aristotle described in *Metaph.* 987a–987b. Although Aristotle famously criticized his teacher Plato for succumbing to "Pythagorean" influence, it is likely that Plato's mathematical philosophy in *De republica* and *Timaeus* was his own innovation rather than a genuine doctrine of Pythagoras and his successors. In particular, Neopythagoreanism was a school of Platonism that tended to elevate arithmetic over dialectics in terms of methodology, and numbers over Forms in terms of metaphysics (see, e.g., Albertson, *Mathematical*

bers not only lead the soul toward the contemplation of the eternal and immaterial truth beyond the material realm—as in Plato's *De republica*[10]—but also constitute the very principle behind all physical reality and even of the ethical and spiritual life.[11]

As Aimé Solignac convincingly demonstrated, it is likely that Augustine had encountered certain Neopythagorean writings by philosophers such as Varro, Cicero, and Nicomachus during his time at Milan.[12] It is not surprising, then, that one discovers elements of Neopythagoreanism throughout his early corpus, most notably in works such as *De musica*, *De ordine*, and *De quantitate animae*. In fact, Solignac could even say that Augustine transmits to us "a sort of Christian Pythagoreanism."[13] Thus, if there is considerable continuity in Augustine's intellectual development, one would expect to find traces of such Christian Pythagoreanism in his more mature works also. Again, *De libero arbitrio* is a particularly interesting work in this regard, since its second book involves a sustained argument regarding *numerus*.

De libero arbitrio is Augustine's final work written in a dialogue form, and it is presented as a dialogue between Augustine and Evodius.[14] As the title shows, the main topic of the book is the freedom of the will. In particular, *Lib.* 2 deals with the questions of (1) how we can know that God exists and (2) whether all that exists is good, in order to show whether free will is good and thereby from God. Augustine outlines the argument in *Lib.* 2.3.7 as follows:

Theologies, 23–39). For a detailed survey of the Neopythagorean tradition of Iamblichus and Proclus, see O'Meara, *Pythagoras Revived*.

10. Plato, *Rep.* 525a–531d.
11. O'Meara, *Pythagoras Revived*, 16–19.
12. Solignac, "Doxographies et Manuels,"120–37.
13. Solignac, "Doxographies et Manuels," 131. Cf. Janby, "Christ and Pythagoras"; and Albertson, *Mathematical Theologies*, 69–80. For a study of an incipient form of a Christian Pythagoreanism of Clement of Alexandria and the Valentinians, see Kalvesmaki, *Theology of Arithmetic*.
14. As Simon Harrison says, however, "[t]he name 'Evodius' . . . is not found in any of the manuscripts and was first printed in Amerbach's version of 1506" (*Augustine's Way into the Will*, 2).

> Let us inquire in this order, if you agree: First, how is it clear that God exists? Next, do all things, insofar as they are good, come from God? Finally, is free will to be counted among these goods? Once we have answers to these, I think it will be quite apparent whether free will was given to humans rightly.[15]

But how does *numerus* contribute to these discussions? First, following a typical Pythagorean line of argument, number demonstrates the existence of an eternal and immutable reality which transcends our rationality, thereby providing evidence for the divine (2.7.20–2.15.40). Moreover, *numerus* proceeds from God and hence is good. Since all created things maintain their forms by the virtue of their being "filled with number" (*numerosa*), all things are thus good and come from God, insofar as they exist. Therefore, free will is good and hence is from God, and sin—caused by the turning away of free will—has no real being. A more detailed exposition of these arguments will reveal the pneumatological character of *numerus* and, as a result, grant us an insight into his intellectual development with regards to pneumatology and Pythagoreanism.

Numerus *and* Sapientia *(2.8.20–2.15.40)*

In the first part of his argument, Augustine attempts to demonstrate the ability of our reason to grasp the eternal and unchangeable Divine nature, through a discussion regarding the immutable nature of *numerus*. To Augustine's question whether one can find anything that all rational minds can see in common, Evodius answers,

> The rationality and truth of number (*ratio et veritas numeri*) is present to all rational beings. ... When anyone perceives it, it is not changed nor transformed, like food, into its perceiver. Nor is there a flaw in it

---

15. *Quaeramus autem hoc ordine, si placet: primum, quomodo manifestum est Deum esse; deinde, utrum ab illo sint quaecumque in quantumcumque sunt bona; postremo, utrum in bonis numeranda sit voluntas libera. Quibus compertis satis apparebit, ut opinor, utrum recte homini data sit* (Augustine, *Lib.* 2.3.7 [*PL* 32:1241]).

when anyone makes a mistake; it remains true and intact, while the person is all the more in error the less he sees it.[16]

Here, following the Platonic and Pythagorean tradition, Augustine presents *numerus* as the exemplary entity that demonstrates the universal, objective, and transcendent reality above our rationality. Augustine then endeavors to refute the Aristotelian conjecture that numbers are merely abstractions from physical objects,[17] by arguing that the intelligible structure of arithmetic operations are not necessarily learned through physical objects.[18] He then further demonstrates the Platonic position on numbers through the observation that one can never truly perceive *one* in the sensible realm, since "no physical object is truly and simply *one*."[19] Nevertheless, we must somehow know *one*, since it is only by knowing *one* that we can enumerate *many*.[20] Moreover, we could not be certain that the law of arithmetic progression holds true for *all* numbers if we only came to know numbers through sense-perception, since they are innumerable; but we are indeed somehow certain that this law is "firm and uncorrupted for all numbers."[21] Therefore, it must be

16.   *ratio et veritas numeri omnibus ratiocinantibus praesto est . . . nec cum eam quisque percipit, in sui perceptoris quasi alimentum vertatur atque mutetur; nec cum in ea quisque fallitur, ipsa deficiat, sed ea vera et integra permanente, ille in errore sit tanto amplius, quanto minus eam videt* (Augustine, *Lib.* 2.8.20 [*PL* 32:1251]).

17.   Aristotle famously argued against the Platonic Academy that numbers do not have a prior, separate ontological existence apart from physical objects that it enumerates. Hence, numbers only exist as dependent on sensible reality, since they are mental abstractions from countable objects (*Metaph.* 1083a–1083b).

18.   Augustine, *Lib.* 2.8.21. But, *contra* Plotinus, Augustine does not necessarily distinguish between the substantial number and the monadic number: here, *numerus* is both mathematical *and* ontological, quantitative *and* qualitative. This is especially significant considering Augustine's distinction between *forma* and *numerus* that will be discussed below. For Plotinus's understanding of ἀριθμός, as well as a summary of the Platonic and Aristotelian theories, see Slaveva-Griffin, *Plotinus on Number*, 56–70.

19.   Augustine, *Lib.* 2.8.22 (Saint Augustine of Hippo, *On the Free Choice of the Will*, 47).

20.   Augustine, *Lib.* 2.8.22.

21.   Augustine, *Lib.* 2.8.23 (Saint Augustine of Hippo, *On the Free Choice of the Will*, 48).

the case that *numerus* and mathematics belong to the intelligible, remaining "pure and unchangeable ... seen in common by all who reason."[22]

Having proven the intelligible nature of *numerus* through standard Pythagorean reasoning, Augustine goes on to support his thesis through the Scriptures: "It is not without reason that *numerus* is connected to *sapientia* in the Scriptures: 'My heart and I have gone around so that I might know and consider and seek *sapientia* and *numerus*' (Eccl. 7:25)."[23] After discussing the "true and unchangeable rules of wisdom,"[24] Augustine then proceeds to consider exactly how *numerus* and *sapientia* are related to each other, and whether *sapientia* is more worthy of admiration than *numerus*. He contends that since *numerus* and *sapientia* belong to the same intelligible realm: "it is indisputable that they are one and the same thing" (*una quaedam eademque res est*). For whenever he contemplates the "residence" (*habitaculum*) or "seat" (*sedem*) of *numerus*, he is "far removed from the body" but must eventually "return—exhausted—to the things of our [realm] (*haec nostra*)," and the same happens when he "thinks most vigilantly and intently" about *sapientia*.[25] Again, he argues from scriptural exegesis:

> Still, since it is nonetheless said of Wisdom in Scripture that it "strongly affects [all things] from the one end to the other and pleasantly ar-

---

22. Augustine, *Lib.* 2.8.24 (Saint Augustine of Hippo, *On the Free Choice of the Will*, 49).

23. *non enim frustra in sanctis Libris sapientiae coniunctus est numerus, ubi dictum est: Circuivi ego et cor meum, ut scirem, et considerarem, et quaererem sapientiam et numerum* (Augustine, *Lib.* 2.8.24 [*PL* 32:1253]).

24. Augustine, *Lib.* 2.10.29 (Saint Augustine of Hippo, *On the Free Choice of the Will*, 54).

25. *Nam cum incommutabilem veritatem numerorum mecum ipse considero, et eius quasi cubile ac penetrale vel regionem quamdam, vel si quod aliud nomen aptum inveniri potest, quo nominemus quasi habitaculum quoddam sedemque numerorum; longe removeor a corpore: et inveniens fortasse aliquid quod cogitare possim, non tamen aliquid inveniens quod verbis proferre sufficiam, redeo tamquam lassatus in haec nostra, ut loqui possim, et ea quae ante oculos sita sunt dico, sicut dici solent. Hoc mihi accidit etiam cum de sapientia quantum valeo, vigilantissime atque intentissime cogito* (Augustine, *Lib.* 2.11.30 [*PL* 32:1257]). Note the similarity to Augustine's description of his and Monica's "vision at Ostia" in Augustine, *Conf.* 9.10.24.

ranges all things" [Wis 8:1]; perhaps the power (*potentia*) that "strongly affects [all things] from the one end to the other" is called *numerus*, while that which "pleasantly arranges all things" is then called *sapientia* in the strict sense, although both are of one and the same Wisdom.[26]

Numerus and *sapientia* can be distinguished in that while even the lowliest beings all have their own numbers, wisdom is only given to rational souls.[27]

But when we contemplate the numbers that we find impressed upon creatures, we realize that they "transcend our minds and remain unchangeable in truth itself."[28] Augustine then offers a very interesting analogy:

> For instance, in a fire one senses brightness and heat as consubstantial (*consubstantialis*), so to speak, and they cannot be separated from one another. Yet the heat affects only what is moved close to it, whereas the brightness is diffused far and wide. Likewise, the power of intelligence that is in *sapientia* warms those close to it, such as rational souls; whereas things that are farther away, such as bodies, are not affected by the heat of *sapientia* but are filled with the light of numbers (*perfundit lumine numerorum*).[29]

---

26. *verumtamen quoniam nihilominus in divinis Libris de sapientia dicitur, quod attingit a fine usque ad finem fortiter, et disponit omnia suaviter, ea potentia qua fortiter a fine usque ad finem attingit, numerus fortasse dicitur: ea vero qua disponit omnia suaviter, sapientia proprie iam vocatur; cum sit utrumque unius eiusdemque sapientiae* (Augustine, *Lib.* 2.11.30 [*PL* 32:1258]). The early Augustine sometimes uses the word *potentia* to indicate the divine persona (e.g., *tripotentem patrem et filiem et spiritum sanctum* [*Ord.* 2.5.16]). This has precedence in the Latin pro-Nicene tradition, namely in Victorinus (see Gerber, *Spirit of Augustine's Early Theology*, 29–31).

27. Augustine, *Lib.* 2.11.31.

28. Augustine, *Lib.* 2.11.31 (Saint Augustine of Hippo, *On the Free Choice of the Will*, 55).

29. *Sed quemadmodum in uno igne consubstantialis, ut ita dicam, sentitur fulgor et calor, nec separari ab invicem possunt; tamen ad ea calor pervenit, quae prope admoventur, fulgor vero etiam longius latiusque diffunditur: sic intellegentiae potentia, quae inest sapientiae, propinquiora fervescunt, sicuti sunt animae rationales; ea vero quae remotiora sunt, sicuti corpora, non attingit calore sapiendi, sed perfundit lumine numerorum* (Augustine, *Lib.* 2.11.32 [*PL* 32:1258]).

Just as a fire's brightness and heat are "consubstantial" and inseparable from one another, so are *numerus* and *sapientia* consubstantial and inseparable. And just as heat affects only what is close to the fire, while brightness affects even what is far away; so is "the heat of *sapientia*" present to only those who are near to itself, whereas "the light of *numerus*" fills all things. Therefore, both *numerus* and *sapientia*—of which "it is certainly evident that each is true and unchangeably true"[30]—inseparably act in unison to reveal the unchangeable Truth (*incommutabilem veritatem*), [31] "which is our God who liberated us from death, that is, from the condition of sin." [32] And in case there was any ambiguity, Augustine later clarifies that this *sapientia* is indeed the eternal *Logos* "begotten by the Eternal Father [Who] is equal to Him."[33]

An Aporetic Conclusion?

David Albertson observes in Augustine, in particular in *De libero arbitrio*, a tension between *numerus* and *sapientia* as competing mediating principles, which eventually leads him to abandon the project of a Christian Pythagoreanism entirely.[34] Albertson reads Augustine as ultimately failing to formulate a resolution between *sapientia* and *numerus* and hence having to "accept an aporetic conclusion"[35] in 2.11.32, which reads,

> Even if we cannot be clear whether *numerus* is in *sapientia* or from *sapientia*, or whether *sapientia* itself is from *numerus* or is in *sapientia*, or whether it can be shown that both are the name of a single thing (*res*); it is certainly evident that both are true, and unchangeably true.[36]

---

30. Augustine, *Lib.* 2.11.32 (Saint Augustine of Hippo, *On the Free Choice of the Will*, 56).
31. Augustine, *Lib.* 2.12.33 (*PL* 32:1258).
32. *et ipse est Deus noster qui nos liberat a morte, id est a conditione peccati* (Augustine, *Lib.* 2.13.37 [*PL* 32:1261]).
33. Augustine, *Lib.* 2.15.39 (Saint Augustine of Hippo, *On the Free Choice of the Will*, 61).
34. Albertson, *Mathematical Theologies*, 69–71.
35. Albertson, *Mathematical Theologies*, 73.
36. *etsi clarum nobis esse non potest utrum in sapientia, vel ex sapientia numerus, an ipsa sapientia ex numero, an in numero sit, an utrumque nomen*

Hence, for Albertson, Augustine's Christian Pythagoreanism remains a tragic "what-could-have-been." His treatment of Augustine's later works is outside the scope of this paper,[37] but in his reading of *De libero arbitrio*, Albertson seems to misapprehend Augustine's logic in 2.11.30–2.11.32. If his logic is not already clear from Augustine's repeated assertion that *sapientia* and *numerus* are "one and the same thing" (*una quaedam eademque res est*),[38] his usage of the particular word *consubstantialis* should be enough to render the logic unambiguous.[39]

Augustine is appropriating the language of *consubstantialis* from Latin pro-Nicene theology, which signifies an absolute *unity and equality of substance* despite a distinction of *Persona* and appropriation.[40] Central to the Latin pro-Nicene tradition—of theologians such as Marius Victorinus, Hilary of Poitiers, and Ambrose of Milan—was the doctrine of *inseparable operations*, that the three divine Personae always act inseparably, because they are of one and the same substance.[41] Thus, the pro-Nicene logic of consubstantiality, applied to *sapientia* and *numerus*, implies that *sapientia* and *numerus* are indeed one and equal and that—despite their distinct appropriations—their operations are ultimately inseparable. Augustine makes this point explicit by stating that they "cannot be separated from one another" (*nec separari ab invicem possunt*).[42] Then, there is no conflict between *sapientia* and *numerus* as separate mediating principles, nor does Augustine believe that they belong to a different *genus*, as Albertson argues.[43] Rather, as light and heat both derive from the

---

unius rei possit ostendi; illud certe manifestum est utrumque verum esse, et incommutabiliter verum (Augustine, *Lib.* 2.11.32 [*PL* 32:1258]).

37. For example, his argument that Augustine's understanding of the Word as *numerus sine numerum* is somehow a rejection of Pythagoreanism is unsubstantiated, especially considering Plotinus's own description of the One as the "measure without measure" in Plotinus, *Enn.* 6.7.32.
38. Augustine, *Lib.* 2.11.30 (*PL* 32:1257).
39. Augustine, *Lib.* 2.11.32 (*PL* 32:1258).
40. For example, see Augustine, *Fid. symb.* 9.16.
41. Ayres, *Augustine and the Trinity*, 43–59.
42. Augustine, *Lib.* 2.11.32 (*PL* 32:1258).
43. Albertson, *Mathematical Theologies*, 73.

same fire and are thus consubstantial and operate inseparably, *numerus* and *sapientia* both derive from the same eternal, immutable, and divine Truth; hence they are consubstantial and act inseparably with this Truth and with one another. Indeed, his conclusion is not aporetic but *apophatic*: it is a confession that "no visible analogy of invisible things can apply in every aspect," instead of an admission that there is an irresolvable contradiction.[44] As one can observe from his other writings such as *De fide et symbol*—written around the same period (395) as *De libero arbitrio*—such apophatic acknowledgment always accompanies Augustine's use of Trinitarian analogies.[45]

A Trinitarian Analogy

The analogy of fire, light, and heat and the language of *consubstantialis* seems, at first glance, to be a Trinitarian analogy, although this particular triad appears to be a novelty in the Latin pro-Nicene tradition.[46] Nevertheless, Ambrose's hymn *Splendor Paternae gloriae*—which Olivier du Roy has identified as a source for Augustine's early pro-Nicene Trinitarian theology[47]—at least identifies the Father with the Sun and the Spirit with its "brightness" (*iubar*).[48] Interestingly, the triad does appear in Ephrem the Syrian's *Hymns on Faith* 40 as an analogy for the Trinity, as well as a similar analogy of sun, light, and heat in *Hymn* 73.[49] John of Damascus also famously uses the analogy of the sun, rays, and heat when describing the Trinity in *On Heresies* 108.[50] Although

---

44. *Non enim ulla visibilis similitudo invisibili rei potest ad omnem convenientiam coaptari* (Augustine, *Lib.* 2.11.32 [*PL* 32:1258]).

45. Augustine, *Fid. symb.* 9.17.

46. To my knowledge, the analogy of fire, light, and heat does not appear in any of the writings by the Latin pro-Nicene theologians prior to Augustine. One could conjecture that Augustine may have received this orally from another pro-Nicene theologian, such as Ambrose.

47. du Roy, *L'Intelligence de La Foi*, 162.

48. Walpole, *Early Latin Hymns*, 35–36.

49. Saint Ephrem, *Hymns on Faith*, 225–28; 349–351. Ayres notes that Ephrem's use of this analogy is "distinct" in the tradition (*Nicaea and its Legacy*, 233–34).

50. Saint John, *Writings*, 162.

it is quite obvious that Augustine could not have been familiar with either the Syriac or the Damascene, they serve as evidence for a hypothesis that the Trinitarian analogy of fire, light, and heat had been transmitted within the pro-Nicene tradition in some form. Moreover, as Isidoros Katsos suggests, in the context of fourth-century Christian metaphysics, radiant light was often identified as the *second hypostasis* of fire and ambient light as its *third hypostasis*.[51] Hence, the most analogous example that one could potentially trace to Augustine—directly or indirectly—is from *Oration* 31 (*Fifth Theological Oration*) of Gregory of Nazianzus,[52] where he mentions the analogy of the Sun, the ray, and the light as he searches for an appropriate analogy for the unity of the three divine hypostases. [53] Considering that the Cappadocian Fathers regarded heat as a property of the radiant light,[54] this may very well have been the source for Augustine's analogy of fire, heat, and brightness. Indeed, Augustine employs the same Trinitarian analogy much earlier in the *Soliloquiorum libri II* (386–387):

> Therefore, just as there are three things that can be noticed—that it is, that it radiates, and that it illuminates—so too in this most hidden God

---

51. Katsos, *Metaphysics of Light*, 168.
52. Gregory Nazianzen's influence on the late Augustine is quite well recognized, for example, in Lienhard, "Augustine of Hippo." In particular, Lienhard notes an "impressionistic parallel" between the *Fifth Theological Oration* and Augustine's *Contra Maximinum Arianum*. Although Rufinus's translation of Gregory's orations did not begin until 399, one could perhaps hypothesize that even the early Augustine may have been directly or indirectly familiar with the analogy from the *Oration*, through an intermediary figure such as Ambrose or Jerome.
53. Gregory of Nazianzus, *Or*. 31.32 (*NPNF*[2] 7:657). Gregory ultimately ends up rejecting this analogy as adequate, for he must "let the images and the shadows go."
54. Katsos, *Metaphysics of Light*, 168. Katsos cites Basil the Great, *Hexaëmeron* 6.8 (*GCS* 103:2–3) and Gregory of Nyssa, *In Hexaemeron* 33 (*GNO* 4.1:15–16).

whom you wish to understand, there are three things—that He is, that He is understood, that He makes all other things understood.[55]

It is particularly noteworthy that here Augustine explicitly identifies the Son as the radiation—which, again, is equivalent to heat in the context of fourth-century metaphysics—and the Spirit as the illumination. The role of the Son as the one making God to be understood and the Spirit's function of "making all other things understood" also parallels the descriptions in *De libero arbitrio* of *sapientia* and *numerus*, respectively.

In any case, it is quite evident that Augustine *is* employing a Trinitarian analogy in 2.11.32. But this raises the question: is Augustine actually alluding to a *Trinitarian theology* of *sapientia* and *numerus*? In other words, are the *sapientia* and *numerus* of *lib. arb.* to be identified with the divine *Personae*, namely the Son and the Spirit? As noted above, the following passage seems to make it clear that at least this *Sapientia* is the Son of God:

> If it disturbs you that *Sapientia* has a Father, according to the hallowed teaching of Christ that we have received in faith; remember that we have also received this in faith, that the *Sapientia* begotten by the Eternal Father is equal to Him.[56]

Then, the language of *numerus* being consubstantial with *sapientia*, the Son, may indeed imply that this *numerus* is none other than the Holy Spirit. In fact, Augustine's description that *numerus* has the same heavenly residence as *sapientia*, where God the eternal Truth resides, seems to support such a reading. An account of a *numerus* or *ratio* pneumatology in the early Augustine—for example in *Ord.* 2—also has precedence in du Roy's work.[57] But,

---

55. *Ergo quomodo in hoc sole tria quaedam licet animadvertere; quod est, quod fulget, quod illuminat: ita in illo secretissimo Deo quem vis intellegere, tria quaedam sunt; quod est, quod intellegitur, et quod caetera facit intellegi* (Augustine, *Solil.* 1.7.15 [*PL* 32:877]).

56. *Nam si te hoc movet quod apud sacrosanctam disciplinam Christi in fidem recepimus, esse Patrem Sapientiae; memento nos etiam hoc in fidem accepisse, quod aeterno Patri sit aequalis quae ab ipso genita est Sapientia* (Augustine, *Lib.* 2.15.39 [*PL* 32:1262]).

57. du Roy, *L'Intelligence de La Foi*, 109–48. Although, as Gerber points out, du Roy is wrong to interpret this just as an uncritical adoption of the

of course, one cannot so easily discount a reading that *numerus* is just another function of the Son, alongside *sapientia*, rather than of the distinct hypostasis of the Spirit. If the *numerus* of *lib. arb.* is a pneumatological category, one should expect to find some language of Personal agency, a clearer distinction between *numerus* from the role of the Son, and correspondence with Augustine's other pneumatological writings from the similar period. Augustine's argument in the following section of *lib. arb.* II provides exactly such evidence.

Numerus *as the Divine Agent of Providence (2.16.41–2.17.46)*

After arguing that *numerus* demonstrates the existence of the eternal and immutable God, Augustine continues towards the next stage of his argument: that all things that exist are good insofar as they exist and hence are from God. He brings attention to another passage of Scripture, namely Wis 6:16: "[Wisdom] appears to them favorably in their paths and meets them in all providence."[58] Augustine's exposition of this passage is worth quoting in length:

> Whichever way you turn, by the footprints (*vestigiis*) imprinted upon its works, [*Sapientia*] speaks to you. When you are slipping away into exterior things by their external forms, it calls you back within; so that you see that whatever delights you in a body, and entices you by your bodily senses, is 'full of number' (*numerosum*). You seek where it is from and return into yourself, understanding that you cannot approve or disapprove of what you come into contact with by the bodily senses, unless within you there are some laws (*leges*) of beauty, according to which you judge the beautiful things that you sense externally.[59]

Plotinian third hypostasis. I ultimately agree with Gerber that there is not quite yet a *pneumatology* of *ratio/numerus* in his pre-Thagaste writings, although I would argue that there is in *Ord.* 2 an incipient seed of the *number pneumatology* that we discover in *De libero arbitrio* (see Gerber, *Spirit of Augustine's Early Theology*, 62–68, 85–90).

58. *In viis ostendet se illis hilariter, et omni providentia occurret illis* (Augustine, *Lib.* 2.16.41 [*PL* 32.1263]).

59. *Quoquo enim te verteris, vestigiis quibusdam, quae operibus suis impressit, loquitur tibi, et te in exteriora relabentem, ipsis exteriorum formis intro revocat; ut quidquid te delectat in corpore, et per corporeos illicit sensus, videas*

Numerus manifests the "divine footprints (*vestigia*)" impressed upon Creation, the eternal and unchangeable aspect of reality that is discovered amongst its temporality and mutability—the trace of the Creator's work hidden beneath each creature's creatureliness. Indeed, every created thing "has being precisely to the extent that they are 'full of number' (*numerosa*)"[60]: *numerus* is what constantly holds them together coherently to maintain their form (*forma*), without which they would cease to exist.[61] This light of numbers (*lucem numerorum*) is also "the internal judge that observes the numbers above" (*interno iudici supernos numeros intuenti*) that prescribes the standard for beauty, as the craftsman applies his craft. It is *numerus* that "moves the craftsman's hands" in a sort of dance that is "full of rhythm and harmony" (*numerose*)[62]— "ask, therefore, what pleases you in dancing; *numerus* will answer to you: 'Here I am!'"[63] In short, *numerus* is the principle of coherence and harmony for all forms and movements. But here, we also observe the description of *numerus* as a Personal agent, who not only judges beauty and animates bodies but also calls attention to itself through its activity, so that the soul may be kindled to draw near to the warmth of *Sapientia*.

---

esse numerosum, et quaeras unde sit, et in teipsum redeas, atque intellegas te id quod attingis sensibus corporis, probare aut improbare non posse, nisi apud te habeas quasdam pulchritudinis leges, ad quas referas quaeque pulchra sentis exterius (Augustine, *Lib*. 2.16.41 [*PL* 32.1263]).

60. Cf. The Neopythagorean philosopher Syrianus's description of the Dyad: "the Dyad *qua* principle is the author of all things of generative power and procession and multiplicity (*plêthos*) and multiplication (*pollaplasiasmos*), and *rouses up all things and stirs them* to the generation of forethought for and care of what is secondary to them, and further *fills all* the divine and intellective and psychic and natural and sensible realms (*diaskosmoi*) *with the numbers proper to them*" (*Syrianus: On Aristotle's Metaphysics 13–14*, 112.35–113.4 [emphasis mine]).

61. Augustine, *Lib*. 2.16.42 (*PL* 32.1263–64).

62. *Numerus* here has an intended double meaning of "number" and "rhythm/harmony," as it does in *Mus*. 6 (see Harrison, *On Music*, 13–16).

63. *Quaere deinde artificis ipsius membra quis moveat; numerus erit: nam moventur etiam illa numerose . . . Quaere ergo quid in saltatione delectet; respondebit tibi numerus: Ecce sum* (Augustine, *Lib*. 2.16.42 [*PL* 32.1263–64]).

When the soul—aroused by the call of *numerus*—recognizes that itself is also "full of number," it realizes that it is only by its internal *leges numerorum* that it can discern the *numerus* outside of itself. Thus, the soul turns its gaze inward to seek the *numerus* within. And by returning into itself, it transcends the sensible realm and sees "the everlasting Number" (*Numerum sempiternum*).[64] Then, "*Sapientia* will shine upon [the soul] from its inner seat and from its hidden chambre of Truth."[65] But when the mind's eye becomes too weak to maintain its gaze upon the *Numerus sempiternus*, the soul may return to the path that Wisdom appeared favorably, to contemplate Her footsteps—the presence of *numerus* as revealed within the created order.[66] As long as the soul remains on the path of *Sapientia*, *numerus* will revitalize the mind's eye so that the soul may seek the vision of *Numerus sempiternus* once more. However, when the soul turns away from the light of *numerus* and towards a shadow, the mind's eye becomes darkened and eventually "unable to see what exists in the highest degree." In such a state, the soul becomes susceptible to evil—which is none other than the turning away from true being.[67]

The immutable *numerus* that gives all beings their coherence, beauty, and being points towards "some eternal and unchangeable Form," Augustine explains as follows:

> Do not doubt, that there is some eternal and unchangeable Form (*formam aeternam et incommutabilem*), such that these changeable things are not interrupted, but with measured movements and distinct variations of forms (*formarum*), traverse through time like poetic verses. This [Form] is not contained in nor diffused spatially, nor is it extended or varied temporally; but through it all [things] are able to re-

---

64. *Numerus sempiternus* most likely refers to the divine nature in general, as "seeing the *numerus sempiternus*" is a description of the beatific vision, rather than specifically referring to the Person of either the Spirit or the Son.

65. *iam tibi sapientia de ipsa interiore sede fulgebit, et de ipso secretario veritatis* (Augustine, *Lib.* 2.16.42 [*PL* 32.1264]).

66. Augustine, *Lib.* 2.16.42 (*PL* 32.1264).

67. *Ex quo incipit non posse videre quod summe est* (Augustine, *Lib.* 2.16.43 [*PL* 32.1264]).

ceive form, and to fulfill and perform the numbers pertinent to the places and times according to their kind.[68]

That is, the eternal and unchangeable Form—which transcends space and time—gives individual forms to each and every created thing, so that every creature may continue to exist by their changing forms and movements through their *numerus*. All changeable things must receive their form, but nothing gives form to itself; hence there must be an immutable and everlasting Form that "while remaining in itself, makes all things new [Wis 7:27]."[69] Augustine identifies this *Forma incommutabilis* as the divine Providence, "through which all changeable things subsist, so that they are fulfilled and performed by the numbers according to their forms" (*ut formarum suarum numeris impleantur et agantur*). And, returning to Wis 6:16, this unchangeable Form and divine Providence is the Wisdom of God "who meets them in all providence." What is notable here is that *numerus* is distinguished from *forma*: the latter defines what sort of being something is, the former how its *forma* remains coherent and moves through space and time.[70]

Since all good things that exist—those that are beautiful by being full of *numerus*—exist by the virtue of their forms, but they must have received their forms from the *Forma aeterna*. Hence, "all good things whatsoever, however great, however small, cannot have their being other than from God."[71] But recall that

---

68. *noli dubitare, ut ista mutabilia non intercipiantur, sed dimensis motibus, et distincta varietate formarum, quasi quosdam versus temporum peragant, esse aliquam formam aeternam et incommutabilem; quae neque contineatur et quasi diffundatur locis, neque protendatur atque varietur temporibus, per quam cuncta ista formari valeant, et pro suo genere implere atque agere locorum ac temporum numeros* (Augustine, *Lib.* 2.16.44 [*PL* 32.1264–65]).

69. *Mutabis ea et mutabuntur; tu autem idem es* (Augustine, *Lib.* 2.17.45 [*PL* 32.1265]).

70. Therefore, Gerber is not quite correct to say that in *Lib.* 2, "[n]umber . . . is a synonym for *forma/species* and is a matter of quality not quantity" (*Spirit of Augustine's Early Theology*, 51). Instead, as he correctly identifies Augustine's eventual distinction of form from order, *numerus* in *lib. arb.* must be identified with order rather than form.

71. *Quamobrem quantacumque bona, quamvis magna, quamvis minima, nisi ex Deo esse non possunt* (Augustine, *Lib.* 2.17.46 [*PL* 32.1265]).

these things only "have forms because they have *numerus*."⁷²
Moreover, this divine Providence "does not permit the movements
of these things, as they deteriorate or advance, from transgressing
the laws of their own numbers."⁷³ At the end of *Lib*. 2, Augustine
summarizes as thus:

> Do not hesitate to attribute to God as its Maker everything in which
> you see measure, number, and order (*mensuram et numerum et ordi-
> nem*). Once you remove these things entirely, nothing at all will re-
> main. For even if some inchoate vestige of form (*aliqua formae ali-
> cuius inchoatio*) were to remain, where you find neither *mensura, or-
> do*, nor *numerus*—since wherever these exist, the form is complete—
> it is necessary that you also take away that inchoate vestige of form,
> which appears to be some underlying material to be completed by its
> Maker. For if the completion of a form is good, the inchoate vestige of
> form is already something good. Thus, if every good were taken away,
> what will indeed be left is not something, but instead absolutely no-
> thing. Yet every good is from God. Therefore, there is no nature that
> is not from God.⁷⁴

Therefore, the *Forma aeterna et incommutabilis* and *numerus*
cooperate as the divine agents of providence: the unchangeable
Forma grants forms to individual creatures and thereby their very

---

72. *formas habent, quia numeros habent* (Augustine, *Lib*. 2.16.42 [*PL* 32.1263]).

73. *motusque ipsos rerum deficientium vel proficientium excedere numerorum suorum leges non sinit* (Augustine, *Lib*. 2.17.46 [*PL* 32.1266]).

74. *Omnem quippe rem ubi mensuram et numerum et ordinem videris, Deo artifici tribuere ne cuncteris. Unde autem ista penitus detraxeris, nihil omnino remanebit: quia etsi remanserit aliqua formae alicuius inchoatio, ubi neque mensuram neque numerum neque ordinem invenias, quia ubicumque ista sunt, forma perfecta est; oportet auferas etiam ipsam inchoationem formae, quae tamquam materies ad perficiendum subiacere videtur artifici. Si enim formae perfectio bonum est, nonnullum iam bonum est et formae inchoatio. Ita, detracto penitus omni bono, non quidem nonnihil, sed omnino nihil remanebit. Omne autem bonum ex Deo: nulla ergo natura est quae non sit ex Deo* (Augustine, *Lib*. 2.20.54 [*PL* 32.1270]). Here, *mensura, numerus*, and *ordo* is from Wis 11:21, a theologically significant passage for Augustine throughout his career. But what is interesting is that this triad is distinguished from *forma*, albeit only in a strict sense. Augustine will later develop this into his doctrine of *rationes seminales* (see Oliver, "Augustine").

existence, and *numerus* sustains their forms by providing laws (*leges*) of coherent and harmonious movement and being. Eternal Form and *numerus* operate inseparably in the divine work of creation and its sustenance.

A Number Pneumatology

Lewis Ayres, following Chad Gerber, characterizes Augustine's early pneumatology as an *order pneumatology*, "which ascribes to the Spirit the function of maintaining created things in their particular individuated and formed existence."[75] For example, in *De vera religione*, written between 390 and 391, Augustine describes the creative act of the Father, Son, and the Spirit towards Creation as follows:

> [E]very intelligent, animal, and corporeal creature, from the same creator Trinity, receives its being to the extent that it exists, has its own form, and is governed by the highest order (*ordinatissime*) . . . Every particular thing or substance or essence or nature, or whatever else you like to call it, has simultaneously about it these three aspects: that it is one something, and that it is distinguished from other things by its proper form (*specie*), and that it does not transgress the order (*ordo*) of things.[76]

A similar idea also appears in *Epistula* 11, written in 389:

> There is no nature . . . and no substance whatsoever that does not have in itself, and does not display before itself, these three aspects: first, that it exists; second, that it is this or that; and third, that it remains as it was to the extent it can. The first reveals the very cause (*causam ipsam*) of the nature from which all things come; the second reveals the form (*speciem*) by which all things are fashioned and formed in a cer-

---

75. Ayres, *Augustine and the Trinity*, 61.
76. *omnis intellectualis et animalis et corporalis creatura, ab eadem Trinitate creatrice esse in quantum est, et speciem suam habere et ordinatissime administrari . . . Omnis enim res, vel substantia, vel essentia, vel natura, vel si quo alio verbo melius enuntiatur, simul haec tria habet; ut et unum aliquid sit, et specie propria discernatur a ceteris, et rerum ordinem non excedat* (Augustine, *Ver. rel.* 7.13 [*CCSL* 32:196–97]).

tain manner; the third reveals a certain permanence (*manentiam*), so to speak, in which all things exist.[77]

The activity of the Spirit that is revealed by this third aspect of nature is the maintenance of creaturely form, and thereby of their existence. Indeed, as Gerber points out, Augustine begins to delineate—without separating—"form" (*species/forma*) from *ordo* in his Thagaste writings; and the role of *ordo* that emerges from his order pneumatology after 389 is "the realization or the sustaining of form in created things."[78] *Epistula* 11 makes it clear that "form . . . is not without reason . . . attributed to the Son."[79] Moreover, the letter concludes with another set of triadic questions: whether it exists, what it is, and how to evaluate it.[80] If the Trinitarian analogy holds, then another aspect of Augustine's order pneumatology would be the Spirit as the absolute standard of approval or disapproval, that is, of beauty, harmony, coherence, and truth.[81]

In discussing his early pneumatology, Ayres also notes that "Augustine frequently hypostasizes *ordo* as that which enables our return to contemplation: 'order is that which, if we hold to it in life, will lead us to God.'"[82] *Epistula* 11 attributes to the Spirit the gift and function of "a certain interior and ineffable tenderness and sweetness of remaining in this knowledge [of the Father through the Son] and of scorning all mortal things."[83] As Gerber summarizes, in Augustine's early writings, "the Spirit is principal-

---

77. *Nulla natura est . . . et omnino nulla substantia quae non in se habeat haec tria, et prae se gerat: primo ut sit, deinde ut hoc vel illud sit, tertio ut in eo quod est maneat quantum potest. Primum illud causam ipsam naturae ostentat, ex qua sunt omnia; alterum, speciem per quam fabricantur, et quodammodo formantur omnia; tertium, manentiam quamdam, ut ita dicam, in qua sunt omnia* (Augustine, *Epistula* 11.3 [*PL* 33.76]).

78. Gerber, *Spirit of Augustine's Early Theology*, 166.

79. *Species . . . non sine ratione . . . Filio tribuntur* (Augustine, *Epistula* 11.4 [*PL* 33.76]).

80. Augustine, *Epistula* 11.4 (*PL* 33.77).

81. Gerber, *Spirit of Augustine's Early Theology*, 177–78.

82. Ayres, *Augustine and the Trinity*, 64 (citing Augustine, *Ord.* 1.9.27 [*CCSL* 29.102]).

83. *quaedam interior et ineffabilis suavitas atque dulcedo, in ista cognitione permanendi contemnendique omnia mortalia* (Augustine, *Epistula* 11.4 [*PL* 33.77]).

ly the divine agent who begins the soul's ascent, causing it to seek the Truth, love its God, and so on."[84] Then, the Spirit of Augustine's order pneumatology not only sustains and animates the forms of creatures but also the soul's contemplation of God. In a sense, these are merely two aspects of one operation, since the proper *ordo* of the soul is the enjoyment of God through *Sapientia*.[85]

If Gerber is correct that in Augustine's early order pneumatology, "[t]he Spirit keeps corporeal things from reaching the formlessness and non-being from which they have been drawn by God, [and] the Spirit also maintains the soul reformed through Wisdom,"[86] perhaps one may also speak of a *number pneumatology* that emerges in *De libero arbitrio*. The similarities between Augustine's early concept of *ordo* and the description of *numerus* in *De libero arbitrio* is quite evident. *Numerus* preserves and animates the forms of all creatures, which has been given by the *Forma aeterna et incommutabilis*—the *Sapientia*, the Son of God. *Numerus*, revealing itself by permeating Creation with its light, also incites the soul towards the contemplation of God through the heat of *Sapientia*. Finally, the inner light of *numerus* within the soul acts as the internal judge of whether something is good—coherent, harmonious, and true—according to the heavenly *numerus* and *Sapientia*. Indeed, when one compares the description of divine Providence in *Lib*. 2.17.46 (that it prevents the creaturely forms "from transgressing the laws of their own numbers") to *Ver. rel*. 7.13 ("that it does not transgress the order of things"), it appears that the concept of *ordo* and *numerus* are almost interchangeable in Augustine's thought, at least in the Thagaste period. Then, considering the "consubstantiality" of *Sapientia* and *numerus*, as well as their heavenly co-habitation, one may very well speak of a pneumatology of *numerus* in *De libero arbitrio*.

As Gerber shows, in the pre-Thagaste writings, Augustine tended to identify *numerus* with Christology—as that of the divine

---

84. Gerber, *Spirit of Augustine's Early Theology* 192.
85. See, e.g., Augustine, *Civ*. 15.22.
86. Gerber, *Spirit of Augustine's Early Theology*, 200.

Intellectus—rather than pneumatology.[87] For example, in *Ord.* 2, Augustine explicitly associates *numerus* with the immortal *ratione desuper*—the Son of God who is the intellectual principle and the archetype behind all things—discerned through the liberal arts.[88] In other words, the Son, as the divine *ratio*, is the very ground of the mathematical order of reality which revealed by *disciplina* of the liberal arts—in particular the *quadrivium*: geometry, astronomy, music, and arithmetic.[89] But the distinct role of the Spirit with regards to this mathematical order was not explicated by Augustine in these early writings.[90]

Recall that in the earliest section of his argument regarding *numerus* in *Lib.* 2 (13.20–13.24), Augustine asserts that the "rationality and truth of *numerus* is present to all rational beings" and that this *leges* is eternal and immutable.[91] If the *numerus* of *De libero arbitrio* is indeed pneumatological, one can see that Augustine now sees the rational structure of the cosmos not only as the work of the Son alone, but as the cooperative work of the Son and the Spirit. Then, one may posit a certain development in Augustine's pneumatology, in which the distinction between his Christology and pneumatology had been further clarified. Now, the Son provides the form of each creature—and of Creation as a

---

87. Gerber, *Spirit of Augustine's Early Theology*, 45–54. Here, I generally agree with Gerber's suggestion of an early "number Christology" in Augustine that appears from *Epistula* 3 and *Ord.* 2, although there does seem to be pneumatological elements already present even in *De ordine*.

88. Augustine, *Ord.* 1.8.25 (*PL* 32.989); 2.14.50 (*PL* 32.1018). See also Gerber, *Spirit of Augustine's Early Theology*, 94–102.

89. Augustine, *Ord.* 2.14.39–2.16.44.

90. Gerber, *Spirit of Augustine's Early Theology*, 162–67, 182–200. Gerber points out that, prior to the Thagaste writings, Augustine did not hypostatize *ordo* as a distinct personal agent. For example, *ordo*, *numerus*, *ratio*, and *forma* are essentially synonyms in *De ordine*. But by the time that he wrote *De vera religione*, Augustine had made the conceptual distinction between *forma* and *ordo* and hypostatized *ordo* as the Spirit. Especially, in *Ver. rel.* 42.79, Augustine had already identified the role of *numerus* as the preserver and the animator of form.

91. *ratio et veritas numeri omnibus ratiocinantibus praesto est* (Augustine, *Lib.* 2.13.20 [*PL* 32.1251]). Augustine had made essentially the same arguments earlier in *Ord.* 2.19.50 and *Immort. an.* 2.2.

whole—thereby granting it its very being, and the Spirit assigns the numbers appropriate to its form, continuously preserving and animating its being. The Son, as the eternal *forma*, is still the very principle and archetype behind the rational order; but it is now the Spirit who sustains this mathematical order as *numerus*. Furthermore, in addition to his early idea of *ordo*, the pneumatological concept of *numerus* now also includes a fundamental principle of *movement*, and hence *life*. Perhaps this also represents Augustine's deepening reflection on the Spirit's role as the Gift and Giver of Life. The distinction that we have observed between *forma/species* and *numerus/ordo* is likely to be a philosophical corollary of this maturing pneumatology; but this distinction is also interesting in itself in view of Augustine's Christian Pythagoreanism.

In the tradition of Neopythagoreanism that Augustine received, numbers were often identified with or compared to the substantial and ideal Forms. But Neopythagoreanism was by no means a monolithic school of thought, since figures such as Nicomachus, Plotinus, and Iamblichus all presented different thoughts with regards to the metaphysical place of number in relation to the ideal Form. Albertson explains that these were the various responses to the perennial problem that plagued the Neopythagorean tradition: the competition between the two mediating principles of the Stoic and Platonic λόγος and the Pythagorean ἀριθμός. [92] For Nicomachus, numbers, together with Forms or "categories," order and structure the material world; in fact, numbers are the very principle underlying even the Forms. [93] As Albertson notes, Nicomachus was able to harmonize λόγος and ἀριθμός as two distinct but "coeval" principles of metaphysical mediation. [94] Responding to Aristotle's argument that numbers have no relation to Forms, Plotinus made a distinction between intelligible (substan-

---

92. Albertson, *Mathematical Theologies*, 46–48, 61–62.
93. O'Meara, *Pythagoras Revived*, 14–23. In particular, O'Meara notes, "Nicomachus' 'categories' are not categories at all (in the Aristotelian sense), but rather Platonic Forms" (17).
94. Albertson, *Mathematical Theologies*, 57–58.

tial) numbers and mathematical (monadic) numbers.[95] The former are qualitative, and the latter—as images of the former—are quantitative and mere abstractions from sensible objects.[96] Moreover, intelligible numbers are the essentially identified with the Forms and belong to the λόγος and the νοῦς (Intellect).[97] Thus, Plotinus effectually eliminated the mediation of ἀριθμός from his metaphysical system, in favor of the λόγος/νοῦς—the second hypostasis.[98] On the other hand, Iamblichus all but subsumed λόγος under ἀριθμός. For Iamblichus, multiple degrees of numbers mediate the entirety of reality: not only the sensible to the intelligible but also the soul to the divine.[99] In addition to the Plotinian intelligible numbers, the "physical numbers" reveal to the soul the very principles—the formal, material, and efficient causes—that order and move the material world; and the mathematical numbers guide the

---

95. Against the students of Plato, namely Pseusippus and Xenocrates, Aristotle argued that since numbers cannot have a separate ontological existence apart from physical objects, numbers cannot be related to ideal Forms. For Aristotle, there is only one kind of number, which is the purely quantitative *mathematical* or *arithmetic* numbers. *Ideal* numbers do not exist, and numbers cannot have any qualitative significance whatsoever. Hence, he concluded, "the arithmetical numbers are monadic" (ὅ γ' ἀριθμητικὸς ἀριθμὸς μοναδικός ἐστιν) (*Metaph*. 1076a–1084a). See also Slaveva-Griffin, *Plotinus on Number*, 58–63.

96. Plotinus, *Enn*. 5.5.4; 6.6.2–4, 9. In particular, intelligible number emanates from the Monad as the principle of multiplicity in the intelligible, constituting a complementary source of multiplicity and being together with the Indefinite Dyad. More specifically, the substantial number is the substantial form which makes something to be one coherent being, instead of a scattered indefiniteness. In comparison, mathematical numbers—like for Aristotle—have little ontological significance, except that they are the quantitative image of the non-quantitative substantial numbers (see Slaveva-Griffin, *Plotinus on Number*, 64–70).

97. Plotinus, *Enn*. 5.1.5; 6.6.10–11. See also Slaveva-Griffin, *Plotinus on Number*, 85–100. As Slaveva-Griffin explains, intelligible numbers are "Being standing in multiplicity" and hence are "ontologically equal and inseparable [with Being]" (*Plotinus on Number*, 90).

98. Albertson, *Mathematical Theologies*, 50.

99. Iamblichus specifically took issue with Plotinus's view of Mathematical (monadic) numbers, which he considered to be still too Aristotelian. Hence, arithmetic as a methodology was much more important for Iamblichus than it was for Plotinus (see Albertson, *Mathematical Theologies*, 62–65).

contemplating soul to the "divine numbers"—the very order of divinity.[100]

Augustine seems to have initially accepted the Plotinian view,[101] relating the intelligible number and Form to the Son—the divine *Intellectus* and the *Verbum*.[102] Augustine also initially followed Plotinus into making the distinction between *numerus intellegibilis* and *sensibilis numerus*, regarding the latter as mere "quantities of bodies" which are in "poverty" compared to the former.[103] But by the time of writing *De libero arbitrio*, Augustine had distinguished the concept of *numerus* from *forma*, regarding them as two distinct but inseparable principles of divine Providence. Moreover, against the Plotinian position, Augustine argues that mathematical numbers are not mere abstractions but have valid ontological existence (2.8.20–2.8.24). Much like Nicomachus, Augustine now conceives of *Sapientia* and *numerus*—the Son and the Spirit—as coeval and harmonious agents of mediation who cooperate to structure and preserve the created order.[104] Hence, Augustine was able to formulate a satisfying *Christian* solution to the Neopythagorean problem of competing mediating principles, by means of the pro-Nicene theology of consubstantiality as well as Scriptural exegesis. Moreover, similarly to Iamblichus, the pneumatological *numerus* serves a spiritual role of guiding the soul toward the *visio Dei*—the *Numerus sempiter-*

---

100. O'Meara, *Pythagoras Revived*, 44–51, 62–66, 79–91. Hence, as Albertson writes, "mathematical operations for Iamblichus amount to theurgic rituals. When properly executed their activities divinize the soul and reveal divine mysteries" (*Mathematical Theologies*, 63).

101. *ut quoniam numerus ille intellegibilis infinite crescit, non tamen infinite minuitur, nam non cum licet ultra monadem risolvere; contra sensibilis* (Augustine, *Epistula* 3.2 [*PL* 33.64]). In particular, his description of the *exitus* and *reditus* of intelligible number (*numerus intellegibilis*) and sensible number (*sensibilis numerus*) from the *Monas* is distinctively Plotinian (cf. Plotinus, *Enn.* 6.6.2–3).

102. Gerber makes this case convincingly in *Spirit of Augustine's Early Theology*, 45–54, 94–98.

103. *nam quid est aliud sensibilis numerus, nisi corporeorum vel corporum quantitas? . . . Et ideo fortasse merito philosophi in rebus intellegibilibus divitias ponunt, in sensibilibus egestatem* (Augustine, *Epistula* 3.2 [*PL* 33.64]).

104. Albertson, *Mathematical Theologies*, 68.

nus.[105] Then, one can observe in *lib. arb.* a certain development with regards to his Christian Pythagoreanism,[106] as he continued to synthesize his appropriation of the pagan philosophical traditions with the teachings of the Scriptures and the pro-Nicene tradition. Indeed, the identification of *numerus* with the Spirit and its distinction from *forma* does appear to be the result of his reading of scriptural passages such as Eccl. 7:25, Wis 8:1, and 6:16 through a pro-Nicene theological lens, namely that of the consubstantiality of the Son and the Spirit and their inseparable operations.[107]

Conclusion

St. Augustine's *number pneumatology* in *Lib.* 2 grants us a glimpse into two dimensions of his intellectual development during the critical period between 391 and 396: the maturation of a pro-Nicene pneumatology and the creative synthesis of a Christian Pythagoreanism. It reveals Augustine's deeply Christian approach to philosophy—in this case, his Pythagorean theory of *numerus*—where his appropriations of pagan philosophical traditions were always normed by his reading of the Scriptures and his reception of the Christian theological tradition. Augustine's *number pneumatology* that emerges from *De libero arbitrio* is that the Holy Spirit preserves and animates the form of all creatures and the whole Creation through *numerus* and guides the soul towards the contemplation of God in the divine *Sapientia*, who works inseparably with the Spirit in providing form and revealing the Fa-

---

105. Indeed, John Milbank has recently pointed out the "theurgic" element in Augustine's Christian Pythagorean theology (see "Confession of Time").

106. Of course, this does not demonstrate in any concrete manner that Augustine was directly appropriating these thinkers. Nevertheless, what is significant is that Augustine's position on numbers has clearly departed from his initial Plotinian view due to his engagement with the Christian Scriptures and tradition.

107. Ultimately, this should not be seen as a radical discontinuity in his thought but rather as a genuine intellectual development in Augustine. The essential elements of this *numerus pneumatology* were already in place from his much earlier writings in the form of the *ordo pneumatology*, albeit requiring some deeper dialectics with his maturing Christian faith.

ther. The modern world, much like that of the Pythagorean imagination, is filled with numbers—in the form of the mathematical sciences, statistics, technology, etc. To the modern readers dwelling in such a world, *De libero arbitrio* reminds us that these numbers are the very "footprints of Wisdom," through which we may perceive the sustaining and life-giving work of the Spirit in order to ultimately contemplate the Wisdom of the Creator. Augustine's beautiful doxology of the *Sapientia*, who is revealed by *Numerus*, seems to be a fitting conclusion:

> Wisdom! The sweetest light of a mind made pure! Woe to those who abandon you as guide and wander aimlessly around your footprints (*vestigiis*), who love your nods instead of you and forget what you hint at. For you do not cease to intimate to us who you are and how great you are; all the splendor of Creation is your nods [toward us].[108]

Bibliography

Albertson, David. *Mathematical Theologies: Nicholas of Cusa and the Legacy of Thierry of Chartres*. Oxford: Oxford University Press, 2014.

Ayres, Lewis. *Augustine and the Trinity*. Cambridge: Cambridge University Press, 2013.

———. *Nicaea and its Legacy: An Approach to Fourth-Century Trinitarian Theology*. Oxford: Oxford University Press, 2004.

Barnes, Michel René. "De Regnon Reconsidered." *Augustinian Studies* 26 (1995) 51–79.

Brown, Peter. *Augustine of Hippo: A Biography*. Berkeley: University of California Press, 2000.

---

108. *Vae qui derelinquunt te ducem, et oberrant in vestigiis tuis, qui nutus tuos pro te amant, et obliviscuntur quid innuas, o suavissima lux purgatae mentis sapientia! non enim cessas innuere nobis quae et quanta sis; et nutus tui sunt omne creaturarum decus* (Augustine, *Lib.* 2.16.43 [*PL* 32.1264]).

Gerber, Chad Tyler. *The Spirit of Augustine's Early Theology: Contextualizing Augustine's Pneumatology*. Ashgate Studies in Philosophy & Theology in Late Antiquity. Surrey, UK: Ashgate, 2012.

Harrison, Carol. *On Music, Sense, Affect, and Voice*. Reading Augustine. London: T. & T. Clark, 2019.

———. *Rethinking Augustine's Early Theology: An Argument for Continuity*. Oxford: Oxford University Press, 2008.

Harrison, Simon. *Augustine's Way into the Will: The Theological and Philosophical Significance of De Libero Arbitrio*. Oxford: Oxford University Press, 2006.

Janby, Lars Fredrik. "Christ and Pythagoras: Augustine's Early Philosophy of Number." In *Platonism and Christian Thought in Late Antiquity*, edited by Panagiotis G. Pavlos et al., 117–28. London: Routledge, 2019.

Kalvesmaki, Joel. *The Theology of Arithmetic: Number Symbolism in Platonism and Early Christianity*. Hellenic Studies 59. Washington, DC: Center for Hellenic Studies, 2013.

Katsos, Isidoros C. *The Metaphysics of Light in Hexaemeral Literature: From Philo of Alexandria to Gregory of Nyssa*. Oxford Early Christian Studies. Oxford: Oxford University Press, 2023.

Lienhard, Joseph T. "Augustine of Hippo, Basil of Caesarea, and Gregory Nazianzen." In *Orthodox Readings of Augustine*, edited by George E. Demacopoulos and Aristotle Papanikolaou, 81–99. Crestwood, IL: St. Vladimir's Seminary Press, 2008.

Milbank, John. "The Confession of Time in Augustine." *Maynooth Philosophical Papers* 10 (2020) 5–56.

Oliver, Simon. "Augustine on Creation, Providence and Motion." *International Journal of Systematic Theology* 18 (2016) 379–98.

O'Meara, Dominic J. *Pythagoras Revived: Mathematics and Philosophy in Late Antiquity*. Oxford: Clarendon, 1989.

Roy, Olivier du. *L'Intelligence de La Foi En La Trinité Selon Saint Augustin, Genèse de Sa Théologie Trinitaire Jusqu'en 391*. Paris: Études Augustiniennes, 1966.

Saint Augustine of Hippo. *On the Free Choice of the Will, On Grace and Free Choice, and Other Writings*. Translated by Peter King. Cambridge Texts in the History of Philosophy. Cambridge: Cambridge University Press, 2010.

Saint Ephrem the Syrian. *The Hymns on Faith*. Translated by Jefferey T. Wickes. FC 130. Washington, DC: The Catholic University of America Press, 2015.

Saint John of Damascus. *Writings*. Translated by Frederic Hathaway Chase. FC 37. Washington, DC: The Catholic University of America Press, 1958.

Slaveva-Griffin, Svetla. *Plotinus on Number*. Oxford: Oxford University Press, 2009.

Solignac, Aimé. "Doxographies et Manuels dans la Formation Philosophique de Saint Augustin." *Recherches Augustiniennes et Patristiques* 1 (1958) 113–48.

Syrianus. *Syrianus: On Aristotle's Metaphysics 13–14*.
　　Translated by John M. Dillon and Dominic J. O'Meara.
　　Ancient Commentators on Aristotle. New York:
　　Bloomsbury, 2006.

Walpole, A. S. *Early Latin Hymns*. Cambridge: Cambridge
　　University Press, 1922.

www.ingramcontent.com/pod-product-compliance
Lightning Source LLC
Chambersburg PA
CBHW060821190426
43197CB00038B/2176